427

Cornell International Industrial and Labor Relations Report Number 13

HEWERS OF WOOD AND DRAWERS OF WATER

Noncitizen Arabs in the Israeli Labor Market

MOSHE SEMYONOV

NOAH LEWIN-EPSTEIN

ILR PRESS

New York School of Industrial and Labor Relations   Cornell University

Copyright 1987 by Cornell University
All rights reserved
Designed by Kat Dalton
Cover photo courtesy of Zionist Archives and Library

Library of Congress Cataloging in Publication Data
Semyonov, Moshe.
Hewers of wood and drawers of water.
(Cornell international industrial and labor
relations report ; no. 13)
Bibliography: p.
Includes index.
1. Palestinian Arabs—Employment—Israel.
2. Palestinian Arabs—West Bank. 3. Palestinian
Arabs—Gaza Strip. 4. Alien labor—Israel.
I. Lewin-Epstein, Noah. II. Title. III. Series.
HD8660.S45   1987   331.6'99275695   87-2682
ISBN 0-87546-132-8
ISBN 0-87546-133-6 (pbk.)

Copies may be ordered from
ILR Press
New York State School of
Industrial and Labor Relations
Cornell University
Ithaca, NY 14851-0952

Printed on acid-free paper in the United States of America
5   4   3   2   1

To Irit Semyonov

and

Marian and Jacob Lewin-Epstein

Now therefore ye are cursed, and there shall
never fail to be of you bondmen,
both hewers of wood and drawers of water
for the house of my God.

Joshua 9:23

Contents

Tables and Figures

Figures

Preface

In the Bible, the story is told of the Gibeonites, who, fearing the people of Israel would do unto them as they did to Jericho and to Ai, dressed in worn garments and shoes, took dry bread and provisions, and went to Joshua to his camp at Gilgal. The Gibeonites claimed to have come from a far country and asked to make a covenant with the people of Israel. Joshua and the men of Israel were persuaded that the Gibeonites had come from afar because they had heard of the fame of the Lord. So the people of Israel made peace with the Gibeonites and made a covenant with them to let them live.

Three days had passed when the people of Israel learned that the Gibeonites were in fact their neighbors and that they dwelt among them. The Gibeonites could not be harmed, for the elders of Israel had made a covenant with them and had sworn unto them by the Lord. So they cursed the Gibeonites, and Joshua made them that day hewers of wood and drawers of water for the congregation.

The term *hewers of wood and drawers of water* is used here symbolically to refer to the lowliest and most servile occupations. Indeed, hewers of wood and drawers of water are found in all societies. Workers in these occupations are destined to remain at the bottom of the social ladder with no real chance of changing their status in society. In modern economies the position of subordinate ethnic minorities and particularly guest laborers is analogous to that of the Gibeonites. In Israel, Arab workers from the West Bank and Gaza Strip occupy the least desirable and menial jobs, and they are frequently referred to as the hewers of wood and drawers of water for Israeli society.

The status of noncitizen Arabs has become one of the most salient social problems facing Israeli society. We undertook the task of studying this phenomenon to understand the process whereby this group has become integrated into the national economy and the impact such integration has had on the social organization of the labor market. Through our work, we hoped to assess a series of theoretical formulations on ethnic stratification in modern labor markets.

Our research was made possible by a grant from the Ford Foundation received through the trustees of the Israel Foundation (grant 12) for the years 1983–85. During the two years of research we were fortunate to have assistance in the organization and analysis of the data from Yasmin Alkalai, Irit Assa, Olivia Blum, Rebecca Raijman, and Haya Stier. We also benefited greatly from the advice and comments of our colleagues Nicholas Babchuk, Judith R. Blau, Yinon Cohen, Harry J. Crockett, Jr., David R. Johnson, Robert L. Kaufman, Vered Kraus, Yehuda Matras, Gershon Shafir, Yossi Shavit, Seymour Spilerman, Andrea Tyree, and Hugh P. Whitt. We are indebted to them and to many others with whom we shared our thoughts and ideas. We would like to thank Frances Benson and Erica Fox for their encouragement during the preparation of the manuscript and for their excellent editorial suggestions.

Some of the findings presented in this book have been reported in *Social Problems* 33 (1986):56–66; *Social Science Quarterly* (University of Texas Press) 67 (1986):411–18; and the *American Sociological Review* 51 (1986):342–51.

Introduction

At the close of the 1967 six-day war, Israel was in control of nearly one million Arabs in the West Bank and Gaza Strip. During the years that followed, an ever-growing number of residents of these militarily administered territories joined the Israeli labor market. Lack of economic opportunities in the West Bank and Gaza Strip made it necessary for many of these workers to seek employment in Israel. As a result, the number of noncitizen Arabs employed in Israel rose dramatically from a few thousand in 1969 to more than 75,000 in 1982. Indeed, Arab workers from the administered territories have become an important source of labor and an integral part of the Israeli economy. By 1982 they had found employment in almost 80 percent of Israel's occupational categories, and they now compose about 7 percent of the Israeli labor force. Throughout this book we will refer to these residents as *noncitizen Arabs* both to keep the description short and to highlight the uniqueness of their position.

Like subordinate ethnic minorities and migrant workers in many industrialized societies, noncitizen Arabs tend to be employed in manual, semiskilled, and unskilled occupations. But not only are they segregated in lower-status, poorly paid occupations; their income is also considerably lower than that paid to Israeli citizens in comparable occupational groupings. Indeed, the influx of Arabs from the administered territories has had significant consequences for the ethnic, social, and economic organization of the Israeli labor market. A study of these workers provides a unique opportunity to explore the dynamic mechanism underlying the integration of a subordinate ethnic group into a national economy.

This study covers the period from 1969 to 1982 and is concerned with the mechanisms governing the incorporation of noncitizen Arabs into the Israeli economy, the status of these workers in the Israeli labor market, and the effect their integration has had on the social and ethnic organization of the labor market. We believe that the contribution of this investigation is twofold. First, on the empirical level, the study entails a systematic examination, the first of its kind, of the process of integration of noncitizen Arabs into the Israeli labor market. Second, on the theoretical level, it discusses the findings in light of sociological theories regarding the dynamics of labor market stratification in ethnically heterogeneous societies.

This book consists of six chapters. Each chapter discusses a topic that touches on a meaningful and significant theoretical sociological issue. The first chapter provides background information essential to understanding the unique position of noncitizen Arabs working in Israel.

The second chapter is concerned primarily with the ethnic organization of labor markets in general and of Israel in particular. Here, we examine the process whereby noncitizen Arabs have penetrated and permeated the occupational system, focusing on the categories of occupations noncitizen Arabs take in the Israeli economy, and especially on changes in their occupational status and rate of occupational segregation.

The third chapter is an inquiry into whether and to what extent the entry of noncitizen Arabs into the Israeli labor market has generated occupational opportunities for other ethnic groups, such as Israeli Arabs, Asian-African Jews, and European-American Jews, already in the system. More specifically, it deals with the question of whether entry of a new ethnic group into an economic system spurs upward mobility across occupations.

The relationship between change in the composition of a labor force and the income of an occupational group is discussed in the fourth chapter. Analysis centers on the question of whether entry of a subordinate ethnic group into an occupational labor market generates competition and thus depresses the income level of workers already employed in the occupation.

The fifth chapter focuses on the socioeconomic gaps between noncitizen Arabs employed in Israel and Israeli citizens. The findings underscore the trade-offs between occupational status and income that noncitizen Arab workers make when they leave the West Bank and Gaza Strip to work in Israel. Such an analysis enables us to discuss the social factors that generate labor migration across economies.

The sixth, and last, chapter is a comparison of noncitizen Arabs in Israel with migrant or guest laborers in other industrialized societies. The findings discussed in this chapter draw attention to the more general process whereby nonresident workers permeate the occupational structure of industrial societies and strongly suggest that Arabs from the administered territories who are employed in Israel are governed by economic and social forces similar to those exerted on foreign (guest) workers in other countries.

Most of the figures and analysis in this study are based on data obtained from labor force surveys conducted periodically by the Israel Central Bureau of Statistics. Separate surveys were conducted for the population of Israel and for the non-Jewish population living in the administered territories. A sample of approximately 10,000 households of Israeli Jews and non-Jews was drawn quarterly, and members were interviewed extensively regarding their demographic and labor force characteristics. Similar interviews were conducted at like intervals with members of approximately 6,500 households in the administered territories. For the purpose of the following analysis, data on individuals from the latter group working in Israel were weighted and combined with the weighted sample of Israelis to generate a complete picture of the work force. This procedure was used for data from 1969 (the first full year that noncitizen Arabs were employed in Israel) and was repeated in 1975 and in 1982. The availability of these data provides us with the opportunity to examine the process from time of contact to the present and to follow closely the emergence of ethnic stratification in the labor market. (Further details on the data are provided in Appendix A.)

1

Social and Economic Forces in Israel's Labor Market

Ethnic Stratification in Israel

Israel represents a particularly illuminating setting in which to examine the integration of subordinate ethnic groups into an economy and the impact of such integration on the organization of a labor market. Israel, despite its small size, is characterized by unusual ethnic diversity (Smooha 1978; Simon 1978; Peres 1971; Eisenstadt 1967). The Israeli population is composed of approximately 83 percent Jews and 17 percent non-Jews. The Jewish population is further divided into two ethnic groups of approximately equal size: Jews of European or American origin and Jews of Asian or African descent. These three groups are organized into a system of ethnic stratification that can be described most succinctly as dual.

> The duality occurs on two levels: Jews and non-Jews (mainly Arabs); and, within the Jewish population, Jews of European or American origin (largely Ashkenazim) and Jews of Asian or African origin (largely Sephardim). In this social system, the Jewish population and the European-Americans comprise, respectively, the upper status groups. . . . A general awareness of these distinctions has led to a popular view of a tripartite ethnic order, with European-American Jews on top, Asian-African Jews in the middle, and Arabs on the bottom. (Semyonov and Tyree 1981, 653)

Non-Jews can easily be labeled a minority in Israel in that they constitute only about 17 percent of the total population. Their peculiar situation is well described by Peres (1971, 1028):

Arabs in Israel are a recent minority. Until 1948, there was statistically a clear majority of Arabs in Palestine, although they had no sovereign power. . . . They are a minority without a political and cultural elite, a village population which had been accustomed to following the leadership of towns such as Jaffa, Nablus, and Beirut. The 1948 war emptied some of these towns and severed the connections with the rest. The resulting lack of trained and accepted leadership increased the vulnerability of the Arabs to Jewish economic and cultural influence.

As a whole, the non-Jewish minority group is lower in all aspects of socioeconomic status than the Jewish population (see, for example, Peres 1971 and 1976; Shtendel 1971; Semyonov and Tyree 1981). Arabs also seem to center in specific occupations and to reside mainly in villages; only a small percentage live in towns. Thus both occupational and residential segregation between Jews and Arabs are extreme (Semyonov and Tyree 1981).

The non-Jewish population is distributed into three major subgroups, with Moslems constituting the largest religious group, Christians the middle-sized group, and Druze the smallest group. This relative order by size of the religious groups has existed since the establishment of Israel as a state in 1948 (Shtendel 1971). Although they all speak Arabic and were influenced by Arab culture, the groups differ from one another in important respects. The main difference is that Christians tend to be concentrated more in urban places and to be better educated than Moslems or Druze. Each religious group is also subdivided into sects; however, this variation is beyond the scope of this study. In the remainder of the book, we will refer to all local Arabs as one group (non-Jews or Israeli Arabs).

The Jewish population in Israel is composed largely of immigrants from a variety of countries. The traditional classification distinguishes between the two geocultural groups: European-Americans and Asian-Africans. In spite of some variation within each group, variations between the groups are considerably greater. Furthermore, the Israel Central Bureau of Statistics distinguishes between these two major categories in its official publications.

The majority of the Jewish population in Israel before statehood was of European-American origin. Most of the Asian-Africans immigrated in the late 1940s and early 1950s, shortly after statehood. The latter group of immigrants arrived mainly from Moslem

TABLE 1.1 *Distribution of the Israeli Population in 1969, 1975, and 1982 by Continent of Birth and Religion*

	1969		1975		1982	
	N (in thousands)	Percentages	N (in thousands)	Percentages	N (in thousands)	Percentages
Jews	2,496.4	85.5	2,959.4	84.7	3,373.2	83.0
Israeli-born						
Father born						
Israel	187.9	16.7	305.5	10.3	532.8	15.8
Asia-Africa	524.7	46.6	718.3	24.3	868.5	25.7
Europe-America	411.8	36.6	482.5	16.3	558.3	16.6
Total	1,124.5	45.1	1,506.3	50.9	1,959.8	58.1
Born abroad						
Asia-Africa	669.6	26.8	653.7	22.1	628.1	18.6
Europe-America	702.1	28.1	799.4	27.0	785.2	23.3
Total	1,371.8	54.9	1,453.1	49.1	1,413.4	41.9
Non-Jews						
Moslems	314.5	74.4	411.4	77.0	530.8	76.8
Christians	73.5	17.4	80.2	15.0	94.0	13.6
Druze and others	34.6	8.2	42.2	7.9	65.6	9.5
Total	422.7	14.5	533.8	15.3	690.4	17.0
Grand total	2,919.2	100.0	3,493.2	100.0	4,063.6	100.0

Source: *Statistical Abstract of Israel*, 1970, 1976, 1984.

countries in the Middle East and North Africa. They were characterized by their limited education, unskilled occupations, and large families. Their economic resources were too small to support their large families and to start new lives in Israel. Furthermore, their orientation to life was traditional; they had minimal exposure to modern Western culture, which dominates Israeli society (Eisenstadt 1954 and 1967; Shuval 1963). Because the Jews who migrated from Moslem countries had to adjust to well-established modern Western culture, which had developed during several decades of settlement in the prestate era, they suffered upon their arrival from multiple disadvantages: limited time in the system, lack of socioeconomic resources, inappropriate cultural orientation, and lack of personal connections.

Although these two ethnic groups are about equal in numbers, veteran European-Americans hold the higher positions in all dimensions of social stratification: income, occupation, education, political power, standard of living, and place of residence (see, for example, Adler and Hodge 1983; Matras and Weintraub 1976; Hartman and Eilon 1975; Smooha and Peres 1976; Yuchtman-Yaar and Semyonov 1979; Yuchtman and Fishelson 1970; Peres 1976; Shavit 1984). Furthermore, the gaps between these two ethnic groups do not seem to have disappeared over the years. They are still evident among second-generation immigrants to Israel. (For details see Hartman and Eilon 1975; Smooha and Peres 1976; Smooha and Kraus 1985; Yuchtman and Fishelson 1970; Nahon 1984.)

Noncitizen Arabs: A New Ethnic Minority

The ethnic structure of Israeli society was somewhat altered during the years that followed the 1967 six-day war. The influx of Arab workers from the Gaza Strip and the West Bank into the Israeli economy created a "new" ethnic group—noncitizen Arabs. As will be demonstrated in the following chapters, this group has become an integral part of the Israeli economy. Its presence has had a significant impact on social processes in Israel.

The increase in participation of noncitizen Arabs in the Israeli labor market was extremely rapid. During the period from 1967 to 1970, only several thousand Arabs from the West Bank and Gaza Strip found employment in Israel. According to the official estimates of the Israel Central Bureau of Statistics, their number reached close to 20,000 in 1970. The rise in participation of noncitizen Arab workers was especially pronounced and intensive during the early 1970s. By 1973 some 60,000 noncitizen Arabs were employed in Israel, representing more than 30 percent of the labor force of the administered territories. This trend continued, albeit at a decelerating rate, into the 1980s. By 1982 the number of noncitizen Arabs employed in the Israeli labor market was more than 75,000. To date about one-third of the Arab work force of the West Bank and the Gaza Strip is employed in Israel. Consequently, noncitizen Arab workers comprise about 5.5 percent of the total labor force in Israel and 8 percent of the male labor force.

The increase in participation of noncitizen Arabs in the Israeli labor market is clearly revealed by the figures in table 1.2. The overwhelming majority of these workers found employment in three economic sectors: agriculture, manufacturing, and construction. Noncitizen Arab workers were overrepresented in these three sectors and considerably underrepresented in all others. Furthermore, their increasing participation in the economy has not affected the extent of overrepresentation or underrepresentation. The overwhelming majority of noncitizen Arab workers has also been male. Females of Arab descent, in adherence to a traditional culture, are much less likely to seek employment in Israel. Because it is impossible to obtain accurate estimates for the small group of female workers, our detailed analysis centers on the male population.

The Social, Legal, and Political Status of Noncitizen Arabs

When Israel assumed control of the West Bank and the Gaza Strip nearly one million individuals resided in these territories. The per capita gross national product in 1968 was IL (Israeli lira) 364 in the Gaza Strip and IL 595 in the West Bank, compared to IL 4900 in Israel. The economy of the West Bank and the Gaza Strip was based on strong ties with the Jordanian and Egyptian economies, and the largest portion of the work force (more than 30 percent) was employed in agriculture. Educational levels of the population in the territories were considerably lower than in Israel. In 1969, more than 50 percent of the adult residents of the

TABLE 1.2 Noncitizen Arab Workers in Israel across Economic Sectors, 1970–84

	Total N^a	Percentage of the Labor Force of Administered Territories	Percentage of Israel's Labor Force	Agriculture		Manufacturing		Construction		Other		Sex (in percent)	
				N	$\%^b$	N	%	N	%	N	%	Male	Female
1970	19.8	11.4	2.0	5.0	5.5	2.3	1.0	10.8	11.9	1.7	0.3	—^{c}	—
1971	33.1	18.8	3.2	7.5	8.1	5.0	2.0	17.4	16.4	3.2	0.5	—	—
1972	50.8	27.2	4.6	12.1	12.6	9.0	3.5	25.3	20.2	4.4	0.7	—	—
1973	59.1	30.7	5.1	11.7	12.5	10.9	3.8	30.8	24.3	5.9	0.9	—	—
1974	66.5	31.9	5.7	13.0	15.5	11.7	4.1	35.1	28.5	6.7	1.0	—	—
1975	63.9	31.5	5.4	9.2	11.3	11.9	4.2	35.2	28.2	7.6	1.1	98.5	1.5
1976	63.2	30.9	5.3	9.9	12.0	12.6	4.3	32.2	27.0	8.5	1.2	—	—
1977	62.0	30.4	5.0	10.1	12.1	13.3	4.5	28.4	24.8	10.2	1.4	97.2	2.8
1979	73.0	34.6	5.5	11.0	13.0	16.7	5.2	34.0	29.0	11.3	1.4	—	—
1980	73.2	34.2	5.5	10.1	11.2	15.6	4.9	35.1	30.4	12.4	1.5	—	—
1981	74.0	34.5	5.4	9.5	10.7	13.7	4.3	38.2	32.4	12.6	1.5	96.9	3.1
1982	76.6	34.3	5.6	10.0	11.9	13.8	4.4	40.9	33.7	11.9	1.4	—	—
1983	84.3	36.3	5.9	10.5	12.4	16.0	5.0	43.3	33.2	14.5	1.6	—	—
1984	86.9	36.0	6.0	12.6	14.9	16.1	4.9	42.8	34.8	15.4	1.7	—	—

Source: Statistical Abstract of Israel, 1976, 1982, 1984.
[a]In thousands.
[b]As a percentage of the economic sector.
[c]Data not available.

administered territories had no schooling and only 17 percent had postprimary education (nine years or more). The corresponding figures for the Israeli population for the same year were 6.7 percent with no schooling and 50.6 percent with nine years or more. These differences in educational levels were clearly reflected in later years among Arabs employed in the Israeli labor market. Half the nonresident Arabs employed in Israel in 1975 had six years of schooling or less, for example, whereas the overwhelming majority of the local population had secondary or postsecondary education. The limited education and lack of vocational and professional skills of the residents of the administered territories had serious consequences when they sought employment. As is generally the case for migrants from developing nations who enter industrialized societies, nonresident Arabs were relegated to nonskilled, menial jobs.

Immediately following the six-day war, the unemployment rate in the administered territories exceeded 10 percent and was one of the main problems facing the indigenous population. Within a few months public works projects were initiated and job opportunities were created in the area, primarily in road construction and forestry. Some 20,000 laborers were employed daily in some form of relief work (Rekhes 1975).

Opportunities, however, were far short of the demand for work, and many Arab residents found no employment. During the first few months employing nonresident Arabs within Israel was strictly forbidden. This policy was guided, in large part, by political and security considerations stemming from the circumstances that had brought the two populations into contact and uncertainty concerning future political developments. In fact, the prevailing belief in Israel at the time was that negotiations would begin shortly which would lead to Israel's relinquishing most of the occupied territory in return for a peace agreement.

An additional and powerful consideration underlay the government policy. In late 1967 and early 1968, Israel was just inching out of an economic recession accompanied by severe unemployment. Arabs from the occupied territories would have directly competed for jobs with Israeli workers. By 1969, however, the employment situation in Israel had improved considerably; the unemployment rate was down to 4.5 percent, and certain economic sectors, primarily construction, agriculture, and manufacturing, had labor shortages. Employers, especially building contractors and farmers, began hiring nonresident Arabs illegally and smuggling them into Israel without official permits. Apparently the economic forces were strong enough to bring about a change in policy, for in July 1968 the government established a policy of controlled admittance into Israel for the purpose of work.

The policy consisted of three major provisions: (1) the number of nonresident Arabs employed in Israel would be limited by a government quota; (2) workers would be required to obtain and carry work permits and could work only for the employer specified in the permit; and (3) both gross and net salaries of nonresident Arabs (including social benefits) would be equal to those of Israeli workers with comparable jobs and skills. To monitor the wage policy set by the government and to ensure continuity in benefits accrued by employees, it was decided that all payments would be made via a payment center. That is, employers would transfer monthly wages to the payment center, accompanied by a list of employees and their earnings. Payment would then be made to the employee after deducting taxes and other payments required of the worker (Rekhes 1975; Amir 1985).

Through the payment center, the government ensured that nonresident Arab employees would be paid basic wages set in collective bargaining agreements between unions and employers. Although this procedure was initiated to guarantee minimum wages, employers have often viewed them as maximum. Employers do not usually provide benefits that are not required by law, such as monthly salaries (rather than daily wages) or raises based on experience, although Israeli workers are entitled to these and additional benefits. Monitoring by the payment center, which emphasizes compliance with the law, thus legitimizes wage gaps between resident and nonresident employees (Shalev 1986).

Except for the quota requirement, these policies have remained essentially unchanged throughout the years since their inception. At first it was intended that the number of nonresident Arabs permitted to work in Israel would be limited to 40,000 to avoid undermining employment opportunities for and benefits achieved by Israeli workers. Israel's economic recovery was rapid, however, and the demand for nonresident Arab workers grew steadily so that by 1972 some 50,000 were employed in Israel and the government abandoned the notion of quota. Instead, it emphasized preference for Israeli citizens over noncitizen Arabs. That is, the intent was that noncitizen Arab workers would be hired only when Israeli workers could not be found for the job.

Organizational Arrangements

The decision to permit Arabs from the administered territories to work in Israel required an apparatus to control and supervise the flow of workers. A network of employment offices (exchanges) was therefore set up in the West Bank and the Gaza Strip. The first seven offices were established in 1968 in the major towns of the West Bank. More than thirty additional offices were put into operation in the following years (Amir 1985). The task of these employment offices was to put Israeli employers needing workers in contact with residents of the administered territories seeking employment.

Employment of noncitizen Arabs in Israel was expected to originate in a request by an employer for laborers. This request was directed to the employment office in the employer's local area. If no Israeli workers with skills to match the job description were available, the Israeli employment office would forward the request to the closest employment office in the administered territories, which in turn would offer the job to registered job seekers with appropriate skills. The worker would then receive a work referral certificate permitting him to be employed by the employer specified in the permit. These certificates had to be renewed periodically, and, according to regulations, a laborer could not change employers without first obtaining permission from the Israeli authorities.

In practice, the process is not as rigid as it may appear. Economic expansion in Israel throughout most of the late 1960s and 1970s was accompanied by full employment and constant demand for workers. Consequently, there developed continuous and free daily movement of noncitizen Arab workers in and out of Israel. In most cases noncitizen Arabs would find work with a particular employer and then legitimize their status; that is, the employment office in their area of residence would issue a work certificate after employment actually began. Furthermore, many noncitizen Arabs apparently bypassed the formal procedures and were employed in Israel illegally.

Based on differences between the figures from labor force surveys and rosters of the Government Employment Service, it is estimated that at least one-third of all the noncitizen Arabs employed in Israel are not registered, and they are referred to as "unorganized." It is within the context of unorganized employment that such economic exploitation as below-minimum wages, substandard working conditions, and the use of child labor is most clearly manifested (Amir 1978a). Employers involved in such practices obviously avoid the payment center and are thus able to pay workers less than minimum wage and do not contribute toward various welfare benefits. Nevertheless, many workers prefer not to register so as to avoid having taxes (and other payments) deducted from their wages and the bother of registering and waiting for work. Although attempts have been made periodically to inspect business establishments or conduct surprise searches for employment certificates, these efforts appear to have been quite benign and the number of nonregistered workers has not diminished over the years. Apparently social and economic forces of the labor market have governed the incorporation of noncitizen Arabs in Israel, despite laws and regulations.

The handicaps suffered by noncitizen Arab workers are similar in many respects to those experienced by migrant or guest laborers in Western Europe during the 1950s and 1960s, by seasonal Mexican workers in the United States, and by temporary African workers in South Africa. Strictly speaking, noncitizen Arab workers do not fit into any one category of migrant labor. (See Rogers 1985 for a comprehensive classification.) Some are seasonal workers who are recruited into agriculture and the canned foods and hotel industries during peak seasons. Most, however, are recruited with no a priori time limitations and thus resemble year-round migrant laborers who are given temporary entry with the option of renewing their permits. Still others are not registered and do not have employment permits and may thus be viewed as illegal workers.

A central aspect of the relationship between noncitizen Arab workers and Israeli society is that these workers are not permitted to live in Israel even when they are employed there. In this respect they are a "commuter" labor force akin to the "frontier" workers (mostly Italians) found in Switzerland, and to a certain extent France, or Mexican commuters to the border states of the United

States. Because of the short distances, most noncitizen Arab workers live in their own communities outside the international borders of Israel and commute to work daily. Their work in Israel does not usually involve change in place of residence. Nevertheless, they share several characteristics with temporary foreign (guest) laborers in other societies. They have moved from an agrarian society into an industrialized economy. They are of distinct ethnic origin and are considered a subordinate minority. They lack citizenship rights and do not benefit fully from the welfare legislation and union protection accorded Israeli citizens. Like other commuters, Arab workers from the administered territories are not permitted to live in Israel and must return daily to their homes in the West Bank or the Gaza Strip.

Finally, Arab residents of the West Bank and Gaza Strip are under military rule and are permitted only limited self-regulation. Opportunities for development in these territories are limited, and the population is largely dependent on Israel in practically all realms of life. Further, the precarious political situation, as part of the broader Israeli-Arab conflict, leads to a general perception of the relationship as temporary. Nevertheless, there is evidence of considerable stability in the employment of noncitizen Arabs within Israel. Of those employed during 1977, 84 percent had worked in Israel for more than two years, and half the workers had been employed in Israel for four years or more. One-quarter of all workers were employed by the same employer for more than three years. According to Amir (1978b), continuity in employment has become a permanent and dominant feature of noncitizen Arab labor in Israel's economy.

2
Ethnic Organization of the Labor Market

The integration of subordinate ethnic groups into the labor market and their location within the occupational structure have long been of fundamental theoretical interest for researchers of labor markets and ethnic stratification. In modern economics labor market stratification is not only an economic but an ethnic matter. Labor market literature is unanimous in the claim that economic sectors, industries, and occupations are segmented along racial and ethnic lines. Subordinate ethnic groups are overrepresented in marginal industries and in the less desirable low-status occupations (Bonacich 1972 and 1976; Baron 1973; Semyonov et al. 1984; Sullivan 1978; Hodge and Hodge 1965; Taeuber et al. 1966; Lieberson and Fuguitt 1967). Nevertheless, sociological explanations regarding the mechanisms that govern the emergence of ethnically segmented labor markets vary considerably.

The simplest and most straightforward explanation of ethnic occupational stratification is presented within the framework of the ethnic succession model (Park 1952; Shibutani and Kawn 1968). According to this model, each group of immigrants enters at the bottom of the occupational hierarchy, taking the least desirable occupations and the poorest paying jobs. As a result, ethnic groups already in the system are pushed one notch up the occupational ladder.

The succession model applies only to periods of economic growth and labor scarcity, however, during which new positions become available for the more veteran immigrant groups. These groups are willing, in turn, to relinquish less attractive jobs to the newcomers (Light 1981). Thus, according to the model, a primitive accumulation process occurs. The position of each ethnic group corresponds to its time of arrival—those who arrived first are on top, latecomers below. Indeed, the succession model in its original form was evolutionary in orientation and did not allow for competition among ethnic groups.

The concept of queuing, introduced by Lieberson (1980), improves upon the succession model. While still using the notion of succession, time of arrival is viewed as only one of many possible bases for stratification of the labor market along ethnic lines. In addition, ethnic groups are viewed as actively competing—albeit with unequal resources—for positions in the occupational hierarchy. According to the queuing model, those ethnic group members who are least desired by employers enter at the bottom of the occupational ladder and are compelled to take the least rewarding jobs vacated by members of superordinate groups. An increase in the number of minority workers generates greater competition for available jobs, but it also provides a larger pool of cheap labor for the least desirable occupations. Thus growth in the relative size of the subordinate group results in larger occupational disparities. This argument fits in well with a long-standing ecological perspective on the influence of compositional changes on race-linked occupational differentiation (e.g., Glenn 1964; LaGory and Magnani 1979; Martin and Poston 1972; Frisbie and Neidert 1977; Wilcox and Roof 1978; Semyonov et al. 1984; Fossett 1984).

The queuing model dovetails with the logic embodied in the two most dominant sociological explanations regarding the relationship between ethnic composition of the labor force and differential occupational opportunities. The earlier view is a social psychological one originally advanced by Williams (1947). Its proponents contend that because it increases job competition between the two groups, a rise in the relative size of a subordinate population generates a threat to superordinates and thus increases occupational discrimination (Blalock 1967; Allport 1954; Williams 1947). As Blalock (1967, 187) said: "Provided that minority competition underlies prejudice, there should be a positive relationship between minority percentage and discrimination."

The other view, known as the "overflow" thesis, centers on the ethnic organization of occupational labor markets. Its proponents argue that occupations are ethnic in composition and that labor markets are split along racial and ethnic lines. An increase in the size of an ethnic minority thus results in a greater supply of cheap labor for economic exploitation (Frisbie and Neidert 1977). Consequently, superordinates benefit from the presence of subordinates; they can abandon the least desirable occupations and move into lucrative, upper-status ones (Cutright 1965; Glenn 1964 and 1966; Spilerman and Miller 1977).

The interplay between labor force composition and differential occupational opportunities is somewhat complicated when a minority group grows and reaches "critical mass." When the group is large enough, members may mobilize resources, develop independent labor markets, and "jump queue" to enter more attractive occupations (Fischer 1975; Frazier 1951; Semyonov and Tyree 1981; Lieberson 1980). But even when "jumping" does not occur, minority groups usually specialize in specific occupational activities and create occupational niches.

> These concentrations are partially based on networks of ethnic contacts and experiences that in turn direct other compatriots in these directions. Each group does this and because the job hierarchy is not a perfect system, such activities help give each group certain special niches that it might not otherwise have in a pure system of queues altered only by ethnic compatriot demands. (Lieberson 1980, 379)

Occupational niches, then, provide "entry ports" into occupations other than those on the lowest rung of the social ladder and hence facilitate activity and advancement of a subordinate group in the labor market (Light 1972 and 1984).

Alternative views focus on exclusionary processes (e.g., Parkin 1979; Taeuber et al. 1966). Proponents maintain that superordinate groups systematically exclude minority workers from the more desirable occupations by using such structural devices as unions, licensing, permits, and formal job prerequisites. Indeed, the notion of a split labor market advanced by Bonacich (1972 and 1976) appears to specify that competition and segregation are temporally ordered processes. According to this view, superordinate groups threatened by wage competition from minority group members establish exclusionary mechanisms to block them from joining lucrative occupations. As a result, the labor market is split along ethnic lines.

In sum, all theoretical approaches are unanimous in the idea that subordinate ethnic groups are typically employed in low-status occupations. Each approach, however, emphasizes different driving mechanisms of change over time. The succession model suggests that a group located at the bottom of the occupational hierarchy will remain in that position unless a new group enters the system and takes over the least rewarding jobs. The status of the subordinate group relative to other population groups is expected to remain constant over time. Theoretical approaches that view competition as the underlying mechanism of change in the position of an ethnic group emphasize the importance of the size of the group and its resources. In contrast, the exclusionary perspective does not specifically identify size as a central factor. Rather, it emphasizes actions taken by superordinate groups to exclude others from higher-status occupations.

Although these theories have been examined extensively in the case of endogenous ethnic and racial minorities in the United States, they have not been applied explicitly to minorities or migrant labor in other societies. For decades, Western European nations have experienced an influx of new migrants. These migrants typically arrive from less developed nations and are of distinct ethnic or racial origin. From a sociological point of view, migrant laborers share many characteristics with other subordinate minorities, and their presence has similar consequences for the social organization of the labor market. Indeed, as Castles (1984) has noted in his book subtitled "Western Europe's New Ethnic Minorities," recruitment of temporary labor and unintended settlement eventually led to the formation of ethnic minorities. While maintaining their subordinate occupational positions, they expanded their involvement in social processes outside the realm of work to include cultural change, the establishment of communities, and political and social conflict. (See also Lewis 1985.) Because the legal and political status of foreigners, especially temporary and seasonal workers, deprives them of many rights enjoyed by citizens, they find the conditions of work even less negotiable than do members of other subordinate groups (Castells 1975; Castles and Kossak 1973; Gorz 1970; Piore 1979).

As noted in the introduction, the conditions experienced by noncitizen Arabs employed in Israel are strikingly similar to those of guest laborers in other industrial nations. Hence the analysis in this work brings the sociological perspectives just outlined to bear on an examination of the integration of noncitizen Arab workers into the Israeli labor market and the impact such integration has had on the economic, social, and ethnic organization of the labor market.

Assessing Occupational Segregation

This chapter examines the mechanisms underlying the entry and permeation of noncitizen Arab workers into the Israeli labor market. We will focus on the occupations available to noncitizen Arabs in Israel, on their occupational status relative to that of other ethnic groups, and on changes in their occupational distribution over time. In general, the analysis assesses the degree of occupational segregation experienced by Arabs from time of entry to the present.[1]

Because our theoretical concern was the social organization of the occupational structure, the units of analysis were occupational categories defined at the two-digit level of classification. Eighty-three occupational categories were identified and matched for the years 1969 (the first year for which adequate information was available on Arabs from the administered territories), 1975, and 1982. (See Appendix B for details.) Each occupational category was given a socioeconomic score (SES) based on Tyree's 100-point index of occupations in Israel, classified at the two-digit level (Tyree 1981).[2]

1. This chapter is not concerned with the question of whether and to what extent variations in the characteristics of human capital (i.e., education, age, occupational skills) are responsible for differences in occupational status and socioeconomic disparities among ethnic groups. These issues will be discussed and analyzed in greater detail in chapter 5. This chapter is mainly concerned with the ethnic structure of the Israeli labor market, the occupational segregation of noncitizen Arabs vis-à-vis other ethnic groups, and changes in occupational segregation over time.

2. Tyree's (1981) 100-point socioeconomic index for Israeli society represents the relative hierarchical standing of each occupational category based on requirements (education) and rewards (income) associated with it. The socioeconomic score is computed as the first principal component loadings of income and education and does not involve subjective perceptions of individuals as to the rankings of occupations. The index was based on data from the 1972 census of population. Although socioeconomic scores computed for the non-Jewish population differed somewhat from scores computed for the Jewish population, the correlation was high ($r = 0.87$). Because different scales could not be applied in the same analysis (Tyree 1981, n. 4), the scores calculated for the Jewish population were used to characterize the occupations. This measure is highly correlated with prestige ratings of occupations but is better suited for comparison over time (Duncan, Featherman, and Duncan 1972) and enables us to examine how the

TABLE 2.1 *Percentage Distribution of Ethnic Groups in Israel by Major Occupational Category and Summary Measures of Occupational Distribution, 1969, 1975, and 1982*

		1969			
Major Occupational Category	Number of Occupations	European-American Jews	Asian-African Jews	Israeli Arabs	Non-citizen Arabs
Unskilled	5	3.2	11.9	22.0	42.1
Semiskilled	24	19.7	30.2	31.3	28.9
Skilled and crafts	30	48.3	48.4	41.3	26.8
Clerical and sales	13	8.4	4.1	1.1	1.1
Professional and managerial	11	20.4	5.3	4.3	1.2
Mean status[a] (standard deviations)	—	41.0 (15.11)	32.5 (11.8)	29.5 (11.1)	25.1 (9.8)
Index of dissimilarity[b] (compared with noncitizen Arabs)	—	70.5	57.5	42.8	—
Index of concentration[b]	—	.85	.84	.76	.60
Index of net differences[c] (compared with noncitizen Arabs)	—	.62	.39	.25	—
N = 100%	83	340,728	254,775	81,752	9376

Note: Because of rounding, figures do not all total 100.
[a]Computed for eighty-three occupational categories weighted by population size.
[b]Computed for eighty-three occupational categories.
[c]Computed for five major occupational categories.

In the first stage of the analysis the occupational status of noncitizen Arab workers was compared with the status of other ethnic groups in 1969, 1975, and 1982. Table 2.1 gives the distribution of four ethnic groups—Jews of European-American descent, Jews of Asian-African origin, Israeli Arabs, and Arabs from the administered territories—for five categories of occupations ordered

different population groups are positioned vis-à-vis one another in the occupational structure.

1975				1982			
European-American Jews	*Asian-African Jews*	*Israeli Arabs*	*Non-citizen Arabs*	*European-American Jews*	*Asian-African Jews*	*Israeli Arabs*	*Non-citizen Arabs*
2.2	8.9	12.2	40.3	2.2	5.8	9.5	37.6
16.3	23.8	33.4	38.4	12.4	19.8	30.4	38.2
43.8	52.1	46.7	20.3	38.6	54.6	46.0	23.1
10.2	5.6	1.8	0.8	10.8	6.7	2.6	0.3
27.5	9.6	5.9	0.8	35.9	13.1	11.4	0.8
44.0	35.3	31.9	24.0	46.6	37.5	33.2	24.5
(16.2)	(12.8)	(10.8)	(8.3)	(16.7)	(13.2)	(12.3)	(8.5)
71.5	57.5	48.5	—	74.0	63.0	51.9	—
.84	.85	.79	.62	.82	.86	.80	.66
.73	.55	.43	—	.75	.59	.46	—
368,518	275,502	92,880	64,096	375,077	320,799	117,111	76,274

by status. Summary measures of occupational standing and segregation are also presented.

The dual ethnic structure of Israel is clearly reflected in table 2.1. Jews are overrepresented in all high-status occupations and are underrepresented in low-status ones. Consequently, the mean occupational status of Jews is substantially higher than that of non-Jews. Within the Jewish population, workers of European-American origin generally hold higher-status jobs than do Jews of Asian-African descent. Israeli Arabs hold higher-status jobs than do Arabs from the administered territories.

The ethnic order of the occupational hierarchy has remained remarkably stable over the years: European-American Jews at the top, noncitizen Arabs at the bottom, and Asian-African Jews and Israeli Arabs between the two extremes. Nevertheless, important changes have taken place in the average occupational status of all ethnic groups. The mean status of the two groups of Jews, as well as that of Israeli Arabs, rose considerably between 1969 and 1982. Each of the three groups improved its status by approximately 10 percent of its mean status at the initial point in time. In contrast, Arabs from the administered territories lost status in both relative and absolute terms.

The decline in the mean occupational status of noncitizen Arabs is even more dramatic when the change in occupational structure is taken into account. Between 1969 and 1982, Israel experienced an impressive upgrading of its occupational structure—the proportion of the labor force employed in high-status occupations increased, whereas the proportion of the labor force in low-status occupations decreased considerably. In 1970, for example, 15.5 percent of the Israeli labor force were employed in professional and technical occupations. In 1980 the figure was 22.6 percent. In contrast, the percentage of the labor force employed in manual (skilled and unskilled) labor declined from 37.7 to 29.7 percent between 1970 and 1980. (See also Lewin-Epstein and Semyonov 1984.)

Evidently the influx of Arab workers from the Gaza Strip and the West Bank into Israel did not find employment in "choice" occupations. On the contrary, the presence of this group in lower-status jobs has increased substantially since 1969, as demonstrated by the percentage distribution and the decline in the mean occupational status of noncitizen Arabs.

The trends we have outlined are further examined and more systematically captured by means of the index of dissimilarity (D) presented in table 2.1.[3] The D values clearly indicate that the

---

3. The index of dissimilarity is defined as $D = \frac{1}{2} \Sigma \mid P_{a_i} - P_{b_i} \mid$ where P is the percentage of workers in occupational category i from ethnic groups a and b respectively. The values of this index represent the percentage of noncitizen Arab workers who would

occupational distribution of noncitizen Arabs is considerably different from that of each of the other groups. The index is especially high when noncitizen Arabs are compared with European-American Jews; more than 70 percent of either group would have to change occupations for equal occupational distribution to be achieved. The figure is somewhat lower, though still impressive, when noncitizen Arabs are compared with Israeli Arabs. Furthermore, in all instances the value of D steadily increased from 1969 to 1975 and to 1982. The figures derived from the index of dissimilarity thus suggest that noncitizen Arab workers have become more occupationally segregated over the years.[4]

A second distributional measure (McFarland 1969) presented in table 2.1—index of occupational concentration—evaluates the ability of an ethnic group to permeate the occupational structure. The measure is based on information theory and the concept of uncertainty.[5] When a person is a member of a group that is distributed across the occupational spectrum, and thus permeates the entire structure, there is much uncertainty associated with identifying the person's occupation even if his ethnic background is known. In contrast, when a person is a member of a group that is restricted to only a very small number of occupational categories,

---

have to change occupations to achieve an occupational distribution identical to that of a second ethnic group (i.e., European-American Jews, Asian-African Jews, Israeli Arabs).

4. Caution should be taken when using the index of dissimilarity for comparisons over time, for it does not control for changes in the occupational structure (cf., Semyonov et al. 1984). Nevertheless, occupational dissimilarities were larger at the later point in time than at the earlier.

5. To measure this uncertainty, or permeability, across the range of occupations we calculate:

$$H = [- \sum_{j=1}^{k} P_{j/i} \ln P_{j/i}] \frac{1}{\ln k}$$

where $P_{j/i}$ is the probability that a person belonging to ethnic group i will be in occupational category j, and k is the total number of occupational categories. If all persons are concentrated in one category, the index will have a value of zero; there is no dispersion. The index obtains its largest value when a group is equally distributed across all categories (i.e., maximum permeation). The value of the index in such a case depends on k—the number of categories—and is equal to $\ln k$ (see McFarland 1969). Thus, by multiplying the sum by $1/\ln k$ as we have, we obtain values that are stated as a proportion of the maximum value achievable, and the measure thus ranges from zero to one. The measure is obviously affected by the definition of category boundaries, for combining two categories into one, for example, changes both the P_i values and the value k. It was shown, however, that when the number of categories approached 100, boundary decision had minimal effect (McFarland 1969).

or, in the extreme, one category, there is little uncertainty involved in identifying the person's occupation when ethnic origin is known.

Turning to the figures in table 2.1, we find that in 1969 European-Americans had the largest permeation value—0.85—indicating the most extensive occupational dispersion across the eighty-three occupational categories. Asian-Africans were close behind with a value of 0.84. Recalling that a value of 1.00 would indicate uniform distribution across all occupational categories, these figures clearly demonstrate the far-reaching presence of Jewish workers throughout the occupational structure. Permeation by Israeli Arabs (0.76) is substantially lower than that of the Jewish population, indicating that this group tends to concentrate in certain occupational categories and to be absent from others. The phenomenon of occupational concentration (lack of permeation) is most pronounced in the case of noncitizen Arabs. The value of permeation for this group is only 0.60.

The index of occupational concentration by itself does not inform us where on the occupational ladder permeation takes place. It enables us, however, to treat occupations as qualitative categories and illustrates differences in diffusion between the groups. When combined with information such as mean status scores, the findings further demonstrate the subordinate position of noncitizen Arabs by quantifying their lack of access to a considerable number of occupations.

A comparison of figures for 1969 with those of 1982 suggests that an interesting process has taken place. There has been a slight decline (0.85 to 0.82) in the index of concentration for European-American Jews, apparently as a result of members of this group leaving the most menial and undesirable jobs. Other ethnic groups, by contrast, permeated the system during this period. Permeation was most noticeable among Arabs whose occupational concentration was the greatest during the earlier period. The figures for Israeli Arabs increased from 0.76 in 1969 to 0.80 in 1982. In the case of noncitizen Arabs, the values increased from 0.60 in 1969 to 0.66 in 1982.

Neither the index of dissimilarity nor the index of concentration is sensitive, however, to differential access in a ranked occupational structure. They do not inform us whether differences in occupational distribution between two groups are systematically related to status ranks. This aspect is captured by Lieberson's (1975) index of net differences (ND), which accounts for the fact that occupational categories are ordered and hence captures the vertical dimension of differences in distribution.[6]

The values of the index of net differences further illustrate the subordination of noncitizen Arabs relative to that of other ethnic groups. When noncitizen Arabs were compared with European-American Jews, Asian-African Jews, and Israeli Arabs in 1969, the *ND* values were 0.62, 0.39, and 0.25 respectively. Thus members of all local groups were more likely to be found in high-level categories than were noncitizen Arabs.

A comparison of the data for the three points in time indicates that major changes took place between 1969 and 1975 and continued, albeit at a decelerating rate, into the early 1980s. The differences increased considerably between 1969 and 1982 for all three comparisons. Patently, the probability that noncitizen Arabs would share the same hierarchical positions as other ethnic groups actually declined.

The figures in table 2.1 illustrate the process whereby noncitizen Arabs permeated the occupational structure and changes in their occupational segregation. Further information, not available from data on aggregate occupational categories or summary measures of occupational distribution, sheds light on the process of occupational permeation from a slightly different vantage point. In 1969, there were fourteen occupational categories in which noncitizen Arabs were overrepresented relative to their proportion of the work force. Eighty-five percent of noncitizen Arabs were employed in these fourteen occupations. In fact, more than 70 percent of this group were concentrated in the following five occupational categories: unskilled and skilled laborers in construction, unskilled

---

6. The measure of net differences (ND) is calculated as

$$ND_{xy} = \sum_{i=2}^{n} X_i \left(\sum_{j=1}^{n-i-1} Y_j \right) - \sum_{i=2}^{n} Y_i \left(\sum_{j=1}^{n-i-1} X_j \right)$$

where X and Y represent distributions of two different groups and i and j are counters used to add up the relative frequencies in rank-ordered categories. The measure indicates which group has a greater probability of occupying higher rungs of the occupational ladder. It takes on a value of 0 when the distributions are equal, a value of 1 when all individuals in group X are higher than all in group Y, and -1 when the opposite occurs.

laborers in agriculture, laborers in fresh food packaging, and laborers in the lumber industries.

By 1982 the number of noncitizen Arabs working in Israel had increased eightfold. They were overrepresented in twenty of the eighty-three occupational categories. In addition to the five occupations mentioned above, noncitizen Arabs were also concentrated in such occupational categories as laborers in the canned food industry, cleaning services, and road construction. Although the participation of noncitizen Arabs in the labor force of Israel has increased considerably, and as a group they have permeated much of the labor market, there are still quite a few occupations from which they are totally blocked. First, there are virtually no noncitizen Arabs in any white-collar or professional occupations. Second, noncitizen Arabs are unable to enter entrepreneurial occupations that require capital or official permits. Indeed, they are not represented in such occupational categories as shopowners, wholesale and retail trade, insurance agents, and marine and aircraft officers. In short, in 1982 noncitizen Arabs were still unable to penetrate nineteen occupational categories out of the eighty-three that were defined.

Table 2.2 lists a selected group of occupations to illustrate the extent to which noncitizen Arabs have permeated various occupational domains. Had their representation been in accordance with their proportion in the labor force we would expect noncitizen Arabs to constitute about 1 percent of all occupational categories in 1969, about 6 percent in 1975, and 8.5 percent in 1982. The figures in table 2.2 indicate rather clearly the differential representation of noncitizen Arabs across occupations.

In occupations such as pharmacists, engineers, and even bookkeepers there was virtually no change during the period from 1969 to 1982. These occupations were not accessible to noncitizen Arabs at the initial point in time and remained so throughout the period. Other occupations, such as auto mechanic, retailer, and electrician, were not available to noncitizen Arabs in 1969 but were somewhat more so by 1982. Nonetheless, noncitizen Arabs were still underrepresented in these occupations in 1982. In yet another group of occupations, noncitizen Arabs were overrepresented throughout the period. Overrepresentation was especially pronounced in such manual occupations as construction and agricultural labor, in which noncitizen Arabs have come to constitute a substantial portion of the work force.

TABLE 2.2 Percentage of Noncitizen Arabs in Selected Occupations

Occupational Category	1969	1975	1982
Pharmacists	0.0	0.0	0.0
Engineers	0.0	0.0	0.0
Bookkeepers and cashiers	0.0	0.0	0.0
Auto mechanics	0.0	4.0	6.0
Retail trade	0.0	0.8	1.7
Electricians	0.0	1.8	2.9
Construction workers	6.0	17.8	25.7
Dyers	0.0	17.4	23.2
Agricultural laborers	7.0	53.0	60.0
(Percentage of the total labor force)	(1.0)	(6.0)	(8.0)

The occupational segregation of noncitizen Arabs in the Israeli labor market and its change over time becomes especially meaningful when it is compared with the occupational distribution of other groups. Only a small number of members of other ethnic groups have been employed in the few occupations in which noncitizen Arabs are overrepresented. In 1969, for example, more than 80 percent of noncitizen Arabs made a living in these occupations compared to 9 percent of European-Americans. Furthermore, the occupations in which noncitizen Arabs were overrepresented were those that were declining. The number of these occupations increased from fourteen to twenty between 1969 and 1982. Yet the proportion of the work force employed in these occupations actually declined (Lewin-Epstein and Semyonov 1984). Apparently members of local ethnic groups have vacated the low-status, declining occupations and moved into the higher-status ones. The participation of a new ethnic group in the Israeli labor force therefore is clearly associated with far-reaching changes in the ethnic organization of the occupational structure.

Determinants of Differential Participation

From the findings reported thus far, a number of conclusions are readily apparent. The occupational segregation of noncitizen Arabs is extreme—they are overrepresented at the bottom of the occupational ladder and are underrepresented in the higher-status occupations. Furthermore, as their participation in the Israeli economy has grown, their occupational segregation has increased and their relative occupational status has decreased.

The literature underscores two central characteristics of occupations that are expected to influence differential recruitment opportunities. The first is the socioeconomic status of occupations. The second is the ethnic composition of occupational labor markets. Students of stratification agree that ethnic minorities are likely to concentrate in the lower rungs of the occupational ladder and are typically blocked from entering higher-status occupations. The socioeconomic status of occupations is defined in this work according to Tyree's (1981) 100-point index.

In addition to the hierarchical organization of ethnic groups, as captured by the socioeconomic standing of occupations, ethnic specialization within socioeconomic categories creates occupational niches. The existence of such niches facilitates intensive recruitment of additional group members to the occupation (Hechter 1975; Lieberson 1980). Thus the ethnic composition of occupations has significant consequences for recruitment regardless of socioeconomic status. The ethnic composition of occupations is measured as the proportion of noncitizen Arabs in each occupation (NCA); the proportion of Asian-African Jews among Jewish working males in each occupation (AAJ); and the proportion of Israeli Arabs in the occupation (ISA).

Other considerations include the following:

(1) The extent to which an occupation is composed of wage or salary earners rather than self-employed workers and entrepreneurs. Subordinate group members typically lack the capital necessary to exploit entrepreneurial opportunities. Furthermore, they face great difficulty in obtaining business permits in the host society. This variable is measured as the proportion of Israeli males who are salaried workers rather than self-employed (SAL).

(2) The occupation-specific unemployment rate, which represents the degree of hardship and lack of security associated with a particular occupation. It has been argued that occupations in the secondary or marginal sectors of an economy are typically characterized by seasonal demand and high turnover (Piore 1979; Sullivan 1978). These occupations are least desirable and are easily penetrated by subordinate groups. This variable is measured as the proportion of unemployed Israeli males in these occupations (UNR).

(3) The age structure of occupations, which reflects patterns of recruitment and retention of labor (e.g., Kaufman and Spilerman 1982; Simpson et al. 1982). An occupation that tends to recruit young workers, for instance, may not hold them as they grow older, and an occupation with an old age structure may have difficulties recruiting young employees. In such higher-status occupations as management, however, age may be a prerequisite. Subordinates who are handicapped in competing with young members of superordinate groups have to settle for jobs characterized by an older age structure. The age structure was defined by the average age of Israeli males in the occupation (AGE).[7]

These occupational attributes serve as a set of independent variables that are expected to explain variation in differential participation of noncitizen Arabs in occupations in 1969, 1975, and 1982 respectively. Differential participation is expressed in terms of cross-product odds ratios. Such cross-product odds ratios represent a unique estimate of the chances that noncitizen Arabs—relative to others in the labor market—will belong to a given occupational group. This measure thus represents the odds at a given point in time of noncitizen Arab workers, relative to Israeli citizens, being employed in an occupational category vis-à-vis all other occupations.

Cross-product odds ratios are defined as $(f_{11} \times f_{22}/f_{12} \times f_{21})$, where f_{11} is the number of noncitizen Arabs in a given occupation and f_{12} is the number of Israeli citizens in that occupation. f_{21} and f_{22} are the respective frequencies of the two groups in all other occupations. For purposes of this analysis the odds ratios were converted into natural logarithms. According to our coding system, positive values indicate odds favoring the employment of noncitizen Arabs in a given occupation relative to Israeli citizens, whereas negative valences show the reverse. This measure is perfectly correlated with the eighty-three interaction terms extracted

---

7. Following the rationale and reasoning provided by Kaufman and Spilerman (1982) regarding occupational age structure, we also distinguished, in a separate analysis, other indicators of occupational age structure such as the proportion of workers under twenty-five and the proportion of workers over fifty in the labor market. These other indicators of occupational age structure did not result in findings different from those obtained using average age structure (reported in the following analysis). Thus, for the sake of parsimony, we preferred to present only findings based on average age as an indicator of the occupational age structure.

from the saturated loglinear model for the cross classification of two ethnic groups by eighty-three occupational categories (Semyonov et al. 1984).[8] This measure (LNCA) is preferable to the simple measure of proportions because it controls for both ethnic composition and occupational structure simultaneously.

The values of the cross-product odds ratios can be interpreted immediately and clearly. In 1982, for example, the odds ratio for employment of noncitizen Arabs as semiskilled construction workers was 4.1. That is, the chances of noncitizen Arabs being employed in this occupation, rather than in all other occupations, was four times greater than for Israeli workers. By contrast, the odds ratio for employment as auto mechanics was 0.37, meaning that noncitizen Arabs were about three times less likely to be in this occupation than Israelis were.

Correlation matrices, means, standard deviations of participation (LNCA), and all occupational attributes included in the analysis are presented in table 2.3. The correlation matrix at each point in time indicates the extent to which occupational characteristics are related to one another and to the rate of participation of noncitizen Arabs in the Israeli economy.

The correlations reveal that occupational characteristics are not

---

8. To make the argument clear, consider a cross classification of occupation by ethnicity. The f_{ij} are the observed frequencies for the ith ethnic group ($i = 1,2$; $1 =$ noncitizen Arabs; $2 =$ others) and for the jth occupational category ($j = 1,2$, where 1 is a given occupation and 2 is all other categories). The proportion of an ethnic group in a given occupational category is P_i (specifically, P_1) where $P_1 = f_{i1}/f_{.1}$ and the proportion of a given ethnic group in the labor force is $P_{i.}$, where $P_{i.} = f_{i.}/f_{..}$. The saturated loglinear model expressed in the previously defined terms is

$$\text{Ln } F_{ij} = \theta + \lambda^E_{(i)} + \lambda^O_{(j)} + \lambda^{EO}_{(ij)}$$

where θ is the grand mean, $\lambda^E_{(i)}$ is the main effect of ethnicity, $\lambda^O_{(j)}$ is the main effect of occupation, and $\lambda^{EO}_{(ij)}$ is the effect of the interaction of ethnic identity and occupation. Equality for this formulation in the distribution of occupations across ethnic groups becomes represented by the model of independence where the $\lambda^{EO}_{(ij)}$ effect is set equal to zero. Setting the log of the cross-products odds ratios equal to zero is equivalent, $\ln (f_{11} \times f_{22}/f_{21} \times f_{12}) = 0.00$. The log of the cross-products odds ratios, $\ln (f_{11} \times f_{22}/f_{21} \times f_{12})$, represents a unique estimate of the chances that NCA ($i = 1$) relative to others ($i = 2$) will belong to a given occupational group ($j = 1$) as opposed to the remaining occupational categories ($j = 2$). Thus positive values indicate odds favoring NCA employment in a given occupation vis-à-vis the remaining ones, whereas negative valences show the reverse favoring Israelis. Zero represents equal odds of employment for the two groups. Using this scheme we were able to examine changes in the odds that the ethnic groups would belong to various occupational categories and the relation of these changes to other occupational characteristics and social trends.

TABLE 2.3 *Correlations, Means, and Standard Deviations of Occupational Attributes in 1969, 1975, and 1982* (N = 83)

Occupational Attributes[a]	SES	ISA	AAJ	AGE	UNR	SAL	$\bar{x}$	s
			1969					
LNCA	−.25	.56	.25	.15	.10	−.16	−1.23	1.29
SES		−.39	−.68	.05	−.38	.10	37.77	15.30
ISA			.39	−.07	.19	−.10	8.50	10.45
AAJ				−.23	.33	.18	42.22	20.67
AGE					−.30	−.39	40.00	6.49
UNR						−.01	2.44	2.58
SAL							71.03	29.74
			1975					
LNCA	−.63	.58	.62	.29	.06	.11	−.94	1.25
SES		−.42	−.72	−.36	−.12	.09	37.77	15.30
ISA			.50	.07	.09	−.16	8.87	9.79
AAJ				.09	.32	.29	42.24	17.41
AGE					−.32	−.35	43.81	5.85
UNR						.32	1.60	1.39
SAL							71.47	15.30
			1982					
LNCA	−.68	.54	.51	.18	.30	.11	−.80	1.43
SES		−.42	−.68	−.10	−.24	.08	37.77	15.30
ISA			.47	−.23	.16	−.15	10.88	11.37
AAJ				−.08	.31	.15	48.75	18.30
AGE					.14	−.13	40.12	5.27
UNR						.09	3.20	3.81
SAL							72.57	25.64

[a]See text for definitions of variables.

independent of one another. Participation of noncitizen Arabs tends to be greater, for example, in occupations in which Israeli Arabs and, to some extent, Asian-African Jews are overrepresented. It also tends to be greater in lower-status occupations, though the relationship is more pronounced in the later periods than in 1969. In addition, the socioeconomic status of occupations

TABLE 2.4 Unstandardized and Standardized Regression Coefficients for Models Predicting LNCA (natural logarithm of odds for noncitizen Arabs) of Employment in Eighty-three Occupations (standard errors in parentheses)

Independent Variables[a]	1969		1975		1982	
	B	β	B	β	B	β
SES	.005	.058	−.029	−.358	−.052	−.557
	(.011)	(.140)	(.010)	(.120)	(.009)	(.102)
ISA	.066	.531	.050	.430	.057	.454
	(.013)	(.101)	(.011)	(.080)	(.010)	(.082)
AAJ	.008	.133	.005	.073	−.001	−.125
	(.009)	(.138)	(.010)	(.130)	(.008)	(.097)
AGE	.041	.207	.044	.206	.065	.240
	(.020)	(.100)	(.019)	(.092)	(.020)	(.070)
UNR	.018	.036	−.059	−.065	.027	.073
	(.053)	(.096)	(.074)	(.080)	(.027)	(.072)
SAL	−.002	−.052	.013	.286	.015	.271
	(.005)	(.110)	(.004)	(.093)	(.004)	(.075)
Intercept	−3.857	—	−3.334	—	−2.779	—
R^2	0.36		0.60		0.66	

[a]See text for definitions of variables.

is negatively related to the proportion of Asian-African Jews or Israeli Arabs in the occupation.

Because the independent variables are interrelated, at least in part, it is essential to estimate the net effect of each variable on the rate of participation of noncitizen Arabs in the labor market. Thus, in the regression equations presented in table 2.4 participation of noncitizen Arabs (LNCA) is taken as a function of SES, ethnic composition, unemployment rate, percentage of salaried workers, and the average age of workers in the occupation in 1969, 1975, and 1982 respectively. The regression equation in column 1 focuses on the initial penetration of the labor market (1969), whereas the two other equations refer to the permeation of the occupational structure at later points (1975 and 1982).

The regression analyses reveal different results for the various points in time. The most striking, and somewhat curious, finding is the lack of a direct effect of occupational status on participation in 1969. The only variables that significantly influenced LNCA at the entry point were ISA and AGE—the proportion of Israeli Arabs in and the age structure of the occupation, respectively. Apparently the penetration of noncitizen Arabs into the Israeli economy took place mainly in occupational niches to which Israeli Arabs had already penetrated and in occupations that had difficulties recruiting young workers.

The results for 1975 and 1982, though similar to each other, are considerably different from those observed in 1969. In the latter periods not only ISA and AGE but SES and SAL affected LNCA. It seems that noncitizen Arabs who joined the labor market between 1969 and 1982 were channeled in disproportionate numbers into lower-status occupations and jobs characterized by higher proportions of wage earners and toward occupations in which Israeli Arabs were overrepresented and the Jewish labor force was older.

The Process of Change

The findings reported thus far consistently underscore the changes in the distribution of noncitizen Arabs across occupations, and especially the decline in their relative status. There are two possible explanations for these changes. First, the dramatic growth in the participation of noncitizen Arabs in the Israeli economy may have been associated with a change in the characteristics of this population. Those who joined the labor market first, on average, were better qualified for higher-status occupations than those who joined later. This explanation was rejected, however, when the years of education, ages, and residences (urban versus rural) of the two populations (1969 and 1982) were compared. The average age of noncitizen Arabs working in Israel did not change significantly over the years. Furthermore, the mean years of education were considerably higher in 1982 (6.7 years) than in 1969 (4.9 years).

The second explanation is rooted in theories of exclusionary processes in the labor market. According to this view, an increase in the size of a subordinate group generates a supply of cheap labor for immediate economic exploitation. Furthermore, an increase in the size of the subordinate group poses a growing competitive threat for jobs. Hence an increase in the participation of noncitizen Arabs in the economy is expected to lead to their intensive recruitment into lower-status jobs.

Had growth in the participation of noncitizen Arabs occurred uniformly in all occupations, one would expect participation to be ordered along a straight line. This equality line is defined by the regression equation predicting the participation of noncitizen

Arabs at a later point in time on the basis of their participation in an occupation at an initial point in time. In figure 2.1 participation is given for selected occupations at two points in time. Participation is defined as the differential odds for employment in each occupation. Thus occupations above the line are those that experienced disproportionate growth in participation by noncitizen Arabs, whereas the obverse is true for occupational categories below the line. Change in differential participation is thus estimated as deviation from the regression (equality) line.

The correlation between participation of noncitizen Arabs across occupations was 0.67 in 1969 and in 1982. This correlation over time indicates a degree of stability in that noncitizen Arabs tended to remain in occupations they initially entered. Nonetheless, participation in many occupations at the later point in time could not be predicted precisely from their initial participation. Indeed, considerable change occurred in the occupational distribution of noncitizen Arabs during this period. The odds of noncitizen Arabs being employed as agricultural laborers, unskilled laborers, and porters grew more than expected on the basis of the initial values. In other occupations the odds declined. These findings applied both for occupations that initially had high odds, such as construction workers and painters, and for those such as electricians and retail trade in which the odds were extremely low.

The following analysis examines the extent to which change in the rate of participation of noncitizen Arabs across occupations was affected by various occupational attributes. This change can be estimated using the following lag model:

$$
\begin{aligned}
LNCA_{(t)_i} = {} & a + b_1 \, LNCA_{(t\text{-}lag)_i} + b_2 \, SES_i \\
& + b_3 \, ISA_{(t\text{-}lag)_i} + b_4 \, AAJ_{(t\text{-}lag)_i} \\
& + b_5 \, AGE_{(t\text{-}lag)_i} + b_6 \, UNR_{(t\text{-}lag)_i} + b_7 \, SAL_{(t\text{-}lag)_i} + e_i
\end{aligned}
$$

In this equation, differential participation at time (t) is estimated as a function of initial participation in time $(t\text{-}lag)$, which represents the stability factor, and other occupational attributes such as SES, ethnic composition, age structure, unemployment rate, and percentage of salaried workers, measured at the initial time.[9]

9. When the lag model is rewritten into an explicit change model, the equation is

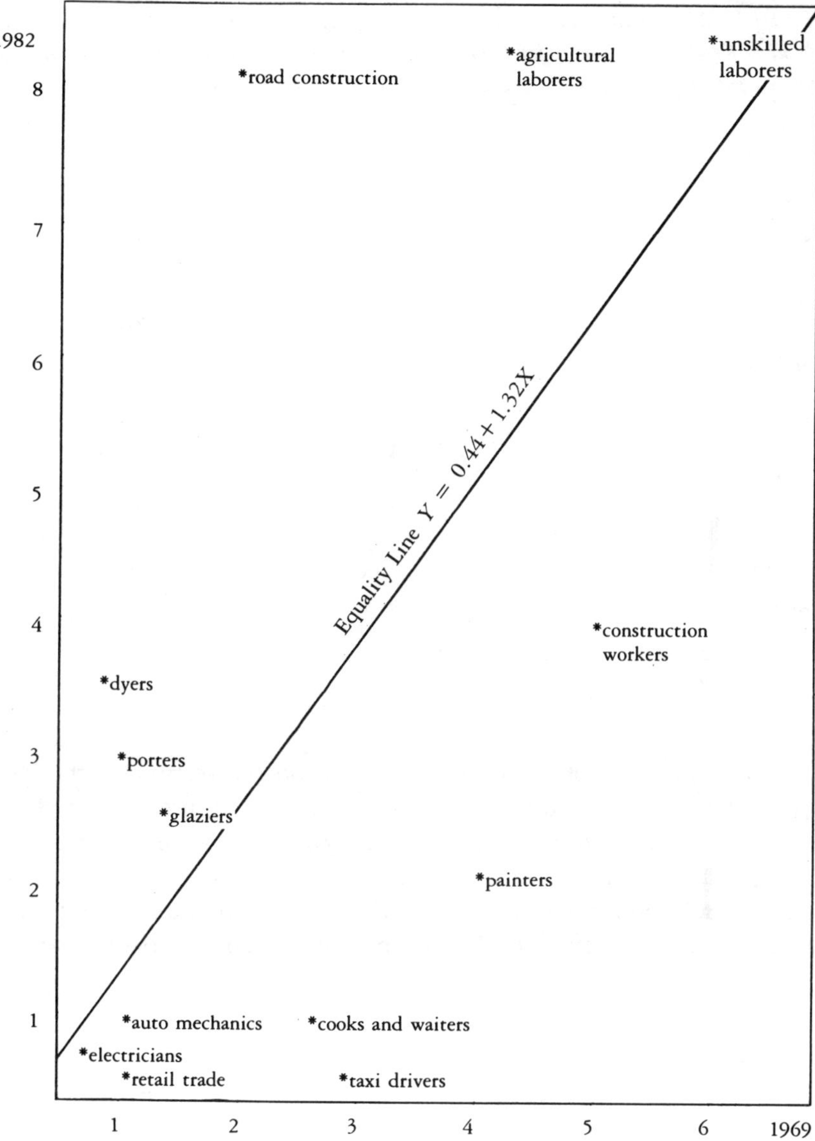

FIGURE 2.1 *Prediction Line for Odds of Employment in 1982 on the Basis of 1969 Values and Odds-Ratio Values for Selected Occupational Categories*

TABLE 2.5 *Unstandardized and Standardized Regression Coefficients for Models Predicting LNCA for Employment in Eighty-three Occupations in 1982, by Means of 1969 Characteristics (standard errors in parentheses)*

Independent Variables[a]	B	β
LNCA, 1969	.280	.253
	(.101)	(.090)
SES	−.057	−.611
	(.010)	(.112)
ISA, 1969	.011	.078
	(.013)	(.089)
AAJ, 1969	−.001	−.017
	(.008)	(.106)
AGE, 1969	.039	.178
	(.019)	(.082)
UNR, 1969	.032	.058
	(.046)	(.078)
SAL, 1969	.012	.262
	(.004)	(.090)
Intercept	−.882	
R^2		.598

[a]See text for definitions of variables.

The coefficients of the regression equation that estimates the lag model for the period from 1969 to 1982 are shown in table 2.5. The results obtained from this regression analysis reaffirm earlier findings, interpretations, and conclusions regarding the process whereby noncitizen Arabs permeated throughout the Israeli occupational structure. As expected, noncitizen Arabs continue to find employment in occu-

---

specified as follows:

$$LNCA_{(t)_i} - LNCA_{(t\text{-}lag)_i} = a + b_1 LNCA_{(t\text{-}lag)_i} + b_2 SES_i + b_3 ISA_{(t\text{-}lag)_i}$$
$$+ b_4 AAJ_{(t\text{-}lag)_i} + b_5 AGE_{(t\text{-}lag)_i} + b_6 UNR_{(t\text{-}lag)_i} + b_7 SAL_{(t\text{-}lag)_i} + e_i$$

Thus, in the implicit change model, the effect of initial participation on change in participation is expressed in terms of the deviation of the coefficient of initial participation $[LNCA_{(t\text{-}lag)}]$ from the coefficient of 1.0 (representing perfect persistence). The other coefficients in the equation pertain to the effect of the independent variables on change in participation, as in the simple form of the lag model:

$$LNCA_{(t)_i} = a + (1 + b_1) LNCA_{(t\text{-}lag)_i} + b_2 SES_i + b_3 ISA_{(t\text{-}lag)_i} + b_4 AAJ_{(t\text{-}lag)_i}$$
$$+ b_5 AGE_{(t\text{-}lag)_i} + b_6 UNR_{(t\text{-}lag)_i} + b_7 SAL_{(t\text{-}lag)_i} + e_i$$

pations into which they initially penetrated. This finding is clearly indicated by the stability factor. Nevertheless, this trend is overshadowed by the intensive permeation of noncitizen Arabs in the occupational system. By 1982, noncitizen Arabs found employment,
though only in small numbers, in many occupations in which they
were not employed or had no access in 1969 (the initial point in time).
This process is clearly captured by the coefficient of $LNCA_{(t\text{-}lag)}$, which
is considerably lower than unity.

In addition, participation of noncitizen Arabs grew in occupations with older age structures and with larger proportions of
salaried workers, even when the stability factor was controlled.
Their participation tended to increase in lower-status occupations.
This negative effect of occupational SES ($\beta = -0.61$) was stronger
than that of any other variable in the model. Curiously, the proportion of Israeli Arabs in an occupation in 1969 had no direct
effect on the participation of noncitizen Arabs in later years.

The weak effect of the lag variable (stability) and the insignificant impact of ISA, coupled with the strong influence of SES,
provide some clues to the mechanisms underlying change. Penetration of noncitizen Arabs into the Israeli labor market was
initially determined primarily by demand in specific occupational
niches. Once noncitizen Arabs had become part of the labor market, their occupational opportunities were determined mostly by
exclusionary processes. These processes, which accompanied their
dramatic increase in numbers, led to their overconcentration in
the lower rungs of the occupational ladder.

The hypothesis that an increase in the number of noncitizen
Arabs who joined the Israeli economy was the prime cause of their
deterioration in status can be further evaluated by comparing
models of change for two intervals. The first period (1969–75)
was characterized by dramatic growth in the employment of noncitizen Arabs. During the second period (1975–82) the rise was
quite moderate. Had a numerical increase been the main determinant of the decline in status, we would expect the negative
effect of SES to be more pronounced in the former period than in
the latter. The regression analyses of the models of change presented in table 2.6 provide firm support for this hypothesis.

The effect of SES on participation in the first time period is twice as
great as in the second period, although the effect in both equations
exceeds twice its standard error and is indeed significant. Apparently

TABLE 2.6 *Unstandardized and Standardized Regression Coefficients for Models Predicting Change in LNCA of Employment in Eighty-three Occupations between 1969 and 1975 and 1975 and 1982 (standard errors in parentheses)*

Independent Variables[a]	1969–75		1975–82	
	B	β	B	β
LNCA at initial time	.324	.334	.865	.757
	(.092)	(.100)	(.083)	(.071)
SES	−.043	−.530	−.019	−.216
	(.009)	(.113)	(.007)	(.078)
ISA at initial time	.007	.057	.004	.031
	(.012)	(.097)	(.009)	(.060)
AAJ at initial time	.003	.052	−.002	−.028
	(.007)	(.110)	(.007)	(.080)
AGE at initial time	.020	.103	.010	.043
	(.017)	(.090)	(.014)	(.062)
UNR at initial time	−.013	−.026	−.010	−.009
	(.042)	(.078)	(.054)	(.051)
SAL at initial time	.010	.235	.004	.079
	(.004)	(.090)	(.003)	(.059)
Intercept	−.557	—	.036	—
R^2	.570		.844	

[a]See text for definitions of variables.

as participation of noncitizen Arab workers in the Israeli economy increased, a larger pool of workers was available to be channeled into lower-status occupations. This trend, though it continued in the latter period, was much more pronounced in the first few years.

Interpreting the Subordinate Role of Noncitizen Arabs

The findings thus far highlight the process of change that took place between 1969 and 1982. Most noticeably, the average occupational status of noncitizen Arabs declined somewhat during the period, whereas that of other groups rose substantially. As a group, noncitizen Arabs drifted away from other ethnic groups in the labor market, as indicated by the various measures of occupational segregation. This process was further underscored in the multivariate analysis, which made it possible to identify two stages—permeation and penetration—in the process whereby noncitizen Arabs became integrated into the occupational system of Israel.

The most conspicuous change during the period under study

was the rapid increase in the number of noncitizen Arabs in the Israeli labor market. Their number increased sixfold between 1969 and 1975 and continued to grow between 1975 and 1982. This growth undoubtedly had an effect on their occupational distribution. In contrast to the central effect of demand during the stage of penetration, the second stage—permeation throughout the system—was affected most noticeably by the socioeconomic status of occupations. The lower the status of an occupation, the larger the proportion of noncitizen Arabs who entered it by 1982. During this second stage, then, it became evident that the new labor group was not a temporary solution to a unique manpower problem. Rather, the relationship became permanent. New mechanisms evolved, which placed noncitizen Arabs within the broader stratification system, relegated group members to low-status jobs, and barred them from others. This change, in which the role of noncitizen Arabs shifted from that of outsiders temporarily engaged to that of more permanent resources, was central in determining the occupations available to them.

The entry process of a new ethnic group into an occupational system, as we have observed, is in fact more complex than suggested by the succession model. Although noncitizen Arabs generally entered in the lower section of the hierarchy, their occupational concentration was not directly related to their low status. Other factors such as the demand for new employees, the existence of ethnic occupational niches, and the tightness of the labor market were indeed more central during the stage of penetration. A view of the process as one of simple ethnic succession is thus incomplete and ignores important dynamic features of ethnic stratification in the labor market.

Distinguishing penetration from the permeation process clearly enabled us to evaluate changes over time. The rapid increase in the size of the noncitizen Arab labor force in the Israeli economy proved detrimental to their position as a group. Occupational differences between them and all endogenous groups actually increased. Curiously, differentiation grew even with respect to Israeli Arabs. These two groups were indistinguishable before 1948, when Israel became a state. Furthermore, as already observed, penetration by noncitizen Arabs was facilitated because there were occupational niches in which Israeli Arabs were concentrated. It might be expected, therefore, that the occupational distributions of the two groups would become more similar. The growing—

rather than diminishing—occupational disparities between the groups suggest that they became separate and distinct entities, at least with respect to labor market activities.

These findings support Lieberson's (1980) proposition, among others (Glenn 1964; Martin and Poston 1972; Frisbie and Neidert 1977; Wilcox and Roof 1978; Semyonov et al. 1984; Fossett 1984), that a large increase in the availability of members of a subordinate ethnic group subjects them to excessive exploitation. Although a subordinate group may at times benefit from an increase in size, it has to reach a critical mass before it can support a fairly segregated labor market. As a group, noncitizen Arabs in Israel did not reach such a mass, and, more generally, such developments are unlikely in the case of migrant workers. In this respect our understanding of the unique position of noncitizen Arabs in the stratification system of Israel was enhanced by introducing the concept of temporary migrant labor.

Noncitizen Arabs are ethnically distinct, are placed at the end of the job queue, and tend to hold the least desirable jobs. Like other minorities, they are a target for economic exploitation. Moreover, noncitizen Arabs find work conditions even less negotiable than other subordinate groups. As a result of their unique legal and political status, noncitizen Arab workers have limited access to capital and to entrepreneurial opportunities. Consequently, they have no alternative but to supply their labor as wage earners.

Our findings suggest important implications regarding the relationship between migrant labor and host societies, to the extent that the processes outlined in this chapter bear upon this broader phenomenon. In the initial stages after the arrival of temporary migrants, their presence is often viewed as specific to occupations or industries with unique labor demands. As time passes, however, both the local and migrant populations realize that the labor market relationship is permanent. It is at this point, when migrant laborers come to be viewed as an integral part of the stratification system, that they are zealously channeled into lower-status jobs. Once part of the occupational structure, they provide a useful solution to recruitment difficulties in less desirable occupations. Thus subordinate noncitizen labor is not incidental to industrial societies but fundamental to their social and economic functioning.

3
Ethnic Group Mobility

Our concern in the preceding chapter centered on the position of noncitizen Arabs in the Israeli labor market. We argued that the position of noncitizen Arabs and its change over time should be assessed in comparison to that of other population groups in the labor market in that the *relative* standing of noncitizen Arabs in the occupational system was of particular interest. In this chapter we maintain this comparative framework but shift our focus of attention. Here we are concerned with occupational change among endogenous Israeli groups. This is not merely the "flip side" of the previous issue. We are not interested in investigating the experience of Israeli workers relative to that of noncitizen Arab workers in the last decade and a half. Rather, we intend to examine and compare occupational patterns of the three major population groups (European-American Jews, Asian-African Jews, and Israeli Arabs). The question we raise in this context is whether the entry of noncitizen Arabs prompted occupational mobility of the local population of Israel and how each of the population groups differentially ranked in the occupational system was affected.

The proposition that entrance of a new subordinate ethnic group into a labor market alters its structure and prompts occupational mobility stems from a long-standing theoretical tradition. Students of race relations have repeatedly noted that the ethnic composition of a labor force has significant consequences on a group's differential occupational opportunities (e.g., Glenn 1966; Lieberson 1980; Semyonov et al. 1984; Spilerman and Miller 1977). Researchers, however, have seldom examined the dynamic relationship between changes in ethnic composition and occupational mobility. In this regard, trends observed in the previous chapter provide us with a unique opportunity to explore this theoretical issue. The purpose of the analysis in this chapter, therefore, is to examine patterns of ethnic group mobility and to distinguish the roles of structural shift and of change in population composition in affecting such mobility. Before turning to the analysis, however, a brief review of the literature on mobility as it relates to ethnic stratification is in order.

Effect of Compositional Changes on Mobility

Theoretical formulations of ethnic stratification have typically been stated in dynamic terms to allow for changes in the position of groups in the stratification system. Proponents of the succession model outlined earlier view social and occupational mobility as generated by the influx of successive groups of immigrants. Each ethnic group enters at the bottom of the occupational hierarchy, taking the least desirable positions. As a result, ethnic groups already in the system are pushed up one notch in the occupational ladder. The position of each group thus corresponds to its time of arrival: those who arrive first are on top, latecomers below. This process is most likely to be maintained when the influx of newcomers more or less equals the rate at which vacancies are occurring in low-ranking occupations. Under other circumstances, however, conflict may arise and the rule of ethnic succession may be undermined (Light 1981).

According to the queuing model (Hodge 1973; Lieberson 1980; Thurow 1975), ethnic groups are ordered on the basis of their desirability by employers. The least desirable ethnic group is thus relegated to occupations at the bottom of the occupational ladder. Consequently, change in the ethnic composition of the labor force has significant effects on a group's differential occupational opportunities. An increase in the relative size of a subordinate ethnic minority usually leads to greater disadvantages for the group.[1] In this regard Lieberson's comprehensive study of black and white immigrants (1980) presented a unique effort to capture system-

---

1. Group size can become an advantage if the group reaches "critical mass" (Lewin-Epstein 1986; Lieberson 1980; Semyonov and Tyree 1981) and is thus large enough to support a semiautonomous market and occupational structure.

atically the changing occupational positions of ethnic groups in the United States. Especially illuminating is Lieberson's comparison of the occupational mobility of white immigrants from southern, central, and eastern Europe with that of blacks in the North. Both white immigrants and blacks fared rather poorly at the turn of the century and were situated at the bottom of the occupational hierarchy. Three-quarters of a century later the position of white immigrants was considerably better than that of most blacks. Lieberson viewed the fact that blacks continued to migrate to the North during a period when European migration was regulated and curtailed as a major determinant of the labor market disadvantages of blacks during this century.

A similar argument is inherent in the "overflow" thesis, which states that as a subordinate ethnic group increases in size, superordinates "overflow" into higher-status positions (Glenn 1964 and 1966; Spilerman and Miller 1977). In the context of the United States it was argued that "so long as most Negroes are employed and subordinated, they will probably continue to reduce the proportion of white workers at the lowest levels" (Glenn 1966, 172). Indeed, the overflow thesis is akin to the queuing model; the former focuses on implications for the superordinate group, whereas the latter highlights the consequences for subordinates. Both models, however, as well as the succession model, emphasize the role of changes in population composition on ethnic group mobility while only implicitly addressing structural changes in the occupational system.

Effect of Structural Changes on Mobility

Students of social mobility have long distinguished structural mobility from pure—or exchange—mobility (Duncan 1966; Hauser et al. 1975; Matras 1980; McClendon 1977; Sorensen 1975). The distinction has frequently arisen in the context of examining mobility tables consisting of the joint occupational distribution of fathers and sons (intergenerational) or of individuals at different stages of their working lives (intragenerational). Because of structural changes in the economy, however, marginal distributions for the two time periods (e.g., fathers versus sons; first job versus current job) usually differ, confounding the interpretation of the tables. Indeed, differences between the two distributions actually "force" a certain amount—and particular patterns—of mobility (McClendon 1977). Such mobility is typically referred to as structural and is defined as "that part of total observed mobility which is directly attributable to changes in the structure of objective mobility opportunities" (Goldthorpe 1980, 73).

The goal of traditional mobility research has been to evaluate the degree of "openness" in a social system for purposes of comparison across nations or over time (Goldthorpe 1980; Hazelrigg and Garnier 1976; Grusky and Hauser 1984; Tyree et al. 1979). Structural mobility is therefore "controlled" so that "pure" mobility can be measured and analyzed. In this context structural mobility has been viewed as a nuisance factor of secondary importance.

The emphasis on "pure" mobility is somewhat unfortunate in that it shifts attention away from important consequences of structural change, a problem recognized and discussed in detail a decade ago by Hauser et al. (1975, 295):

> Rather than treating shifts in the occupational structure as a nuisance factor, to be set aside before undertaking comparative mobility analysis, we suggest that shifts in the occupational structure may be both the driving force and the problematic issue in comparative mobility studies.

Simkus (1984) and Robinson (1984) explicitly addressed the question of how structural shifts associated with industrialization result in constraints on occupational mobility over time. Simkus identified several distinct components of these constraints, which he referred to as discrepancy, concentration, and composition effects. Each offers a unique contribution to the explanation of the process of mobility. Discrepancy refers to differences in the marginal distributions of occupations at two points in time, which lead to "forced" mobility. Concentration is defined as the extent to which occupational distributions depart from equiproportional distributions. The composition component captures the varying inheritance patterns typical of some occupational categories. Shifts in the occupational structure (discrepancy) appear to have the greatest impact on mobility. As Simkus said (1984, 305): "While shifting discrepancy effects do not constitute the whole story of structural changes in intergenerational mobility, they play a leading role in the highest rates observed in modern societies."

Occupational mobility, whether pure or structural, has been researched extensively. Surprisingly, ethnic group mobility has received little, if any, attention in this context. Several studies (Featherman and Hauser 1976; Hauser and Featherman 1977; Hout 1984) explore the mobility of individuals from particular ethnic backgrounds, but none examines changes in the structure of ethnic stratification. This neglect is especially curious insofar as mobility appears to be a central theme in the literature on ethnic stratification (Lieberson 1970 and 1980).

Noncitizen Arabs and Ethnic Group Mobility

A number of issues concerning ethnic group mobility emerge from the previous discussion. First and foremost is whether and in what ways the hierarchical relationship between ethnic groups in the labor market is altered over time. Second is the need to separate the effects of structural shifts from those of change in the composition of the labor force. Israel appears to be a near ideal natural setting for considering such issues.

In discussing mobility in the present context we are referring to the aggregate net changes that take place in the occupational distribution of a group and not to the movement of individuals per se. Hence, when we examine change in the representation of a particular ethnic group in an occupation, we are not concerned with identifying which individuals remained in the occupation, which ones entered, where those who left the occupation went, and so on. Rather, our aim is to identify patterns of relative growth and contraction in the representation of ethnic groups in particular categories and to examine these patterns in view of various characteristics of the occupations.

The situation in Israel in recent years has led to the belief among the public that the entry of noncitizen Arabs has generated upward occupational mobility among all native endogenous ethnic groups. This notion is captured in a monologue of a North African Jew recorded by the famous Israeli novelist Amos Oz (1983, 36):

If they give back the territories the Arabs will stop coming to work, and then and there you'll put us back into the dead-end jobs like before. . . . Look at my daughter; she works in a bank now, and every evening an Arab comes to clean the building. All you want is to dump her from the bank into some textile factory, or have her wash the floor instead of the Arab.

The following analysis will examine the extent to which occupational mobility in Israel was prompted by structural shifts in the economy and by change in the ethnic composition of the work force. The analysis centers in particular on the effect the entry of noncitizen Arabs has had on the occupational mobility of endogenous groups.

Overview

During the years following the six-day war Israel experienced substantial changes in the ethnic and occupational structure of its labor force. Table 3.1 displays the distribution of four ethnic groups—Jews of European-American origin, Jews of Asian-African origin, Israeli Arabs, and noncitizen Arabs—across ten major occupational categories.[2] Data are provided here in greater detail than in chapter 2 to give the reader better insight into occupational differences among the groups. Once again the ethnic structure of Israel is clearly mirrored in the figures.[3] Jews, especially of European-American descent, have been overrepresented in professional and scientific occupations and in managerial and clerical jobs. Arabs, both Israeli and noncitizen, have been overrepresented in agricultural and construction occupations. Consequently, the mean occupational status of Jews has been substantially higher than that of non-Jews. Within the Jewish population European-American Jews have been overrepresented in the professional and managerial occupations, whereas Asian-African Jews have tended to concentrate in blue-collar and service occupations. Noncitizen Arabs have held mostly agricultural, semiskilled, and unskilled jobs and generally have been located at the bottom of the occupational hierarchy.

A number of conclusions are readily apparent from the com-

2. The occupational classification used by the Israel Central Bureau of Statistics was modified in 1972. Consequently, occupational distributions for the years 1969 and 1982 could not be compared directly. Because we were interested specifically in comparisons over time, the 1982 data were reclassified according to the two-digit occupational categories available for 1969 data.

3. Although differences in fertility contributed somewhat to change in the relative

TABLE 3.1 Occupational Distribution and Mean Status of Males in Israel in 1969 and 1982, by Ethnic Group (percentages)

Occupational Group	Number of Occupations	Mean Status Score	1969					1982				
			Total	European-American Jews	Asian-African Jews	Israeli Arabs	Noncitizen Arabs	Total	European-American Jews	Asian-African Jews	Israeli Arabs	Noncitizen Arabs
Professional, scientific, and technical	10	64.5	10.3	15.6	5.5	3.9	1.5	15.9	26.5	9.0	10.0	0.8
Managerial and clerical	6	47.8	14.6	21.5	9.3	3.6	0.4	15.6	22.3	14.1	5.6	0.4
Skilled workers in transport and communications	10	41.3	7.2	7.5	7.3	6.2	3.1	7.4	5.8	10.0	9.0	1.0
Trade and sales workers	7	39.4	8.1	8.6	7.5	7.9	3.8	7.9	8.2	8.6	8.8	2.2
Craftsmen	8	36.9	10.9	10.1	13.0	7.9	12.3	9.4	7.0	11.3	12.8	7.7
Construction and kindred workers	8	31.3	9.3	4.9	10.7	20.2	45.0	9.5	2.8	8.5	15.6	41.0
Agricultural workers	8	30.4	10.9	8.1	10.1	24.0	20.8	7.3	6.1	6.1	11.2	12.2
Service workers	10	28.8	8.8	6.3	11.8	10.0	6.5	8.5	6.1	10.6	9.8	9.7

Table 3.1 *(continued)*

Occupational Group	Number of Occupations	Mean Status Score	1969					1982				
			Total	European-American Jews	Asian-African Jews	Israeli Arabs	Noncitizen Arabs	Total	European-American Jews	Asian-African Jews	Israeli Arabs	Noncitizen Arabs
Semiskilled workers	8	28.0	6.0	8.2	4.5	5.7	3.1	6.5	4.8	6.6	6.0	17.0
Unskilled workers	8	26.7	13.9	16.6	12.9	10.6	3.5	12.0	10.4	15.2	11.2	8.0
N	83		24,295	9,041	12,091	2,903	260	28,933	12,318	10,536	3,845	2,234
Percent of total			100.0	37.2	49.8	11.9	1.1	100.0	42.6	36.4	13.3	7.7
Mean status			36.3	32.5	41.0	29.5	25.1	39.8	46.6	37.5	33.2	24.5

parisons over time in table 3.1. First, the relative order of ethnic groups in the occupational structure remained remarkably stable during the period. Second, Israel experienced an impressive occupational upgrading. The proportion of the labor force employed in high-status occupations (i.e., professional, scientific, and technical jobs) grew from 10.3 percent to 15.9 percent. In contrast, the proportion of the work force in agricultural and manual jobs declined considerably. Further changes occurred within these broad categories so that higher-status occupations tended to expand.

Third, important changes took place in the occupational distribution of each ethnic group. The mean occupational status (Tyree's [1981] SES scale) of European-American Jews, Asian-African Jews, and Israeli Arabs improved by approximately 10 percent of their initial status. In contrast, the occupational status of noncitizen Arabs did not improve; if anything, it declined in both relative and absolute terms.

It should be emphasized that these figures do not negate the fact that certain individuals improved their occupational standing during the years they were employed in Israel. Some noncitizen Arabs have been employed in Israel for more than fifteen years. They started as unskilled laborers in construction and worked their way into skilled jobs in this industry. Others, working in manufacturing, have become machine operators. As a rule, however, these workers did not attain positions of authority, and, more important, the upward mobility of particular individuals was countered by an increase in the number of noncitizen Arabs in the lowest occupational categories, resulting in a slight decline in the average occupational standing of the group.

Because a variety of changes took place during the period from 1969 to 1982, it is not clear to what extent the upward occupational mobility of the three endogenous ethnic groups was determined by shifts in the occupational structure, entry and growth of a subordinate ethnic group, or both. This question will be examined in the loglinear analysis that follows.

---

size of European-American and Asian-African Jewish groups vis-à-vis one another, the large increase in the proportion of non-Jews was primarily a result of changing patterns of employment and participation in Israel's labor market.

Assessing Structural and Compositional Changes

The issue raised in the preceding section can be stated most succinctly as whether the relationship between ethnicity and occupation changed during the period under study. In this form the issue can be examined by means of the loglinear model for the joint distribution of ethnicity, occupation, and time. The model is estimated here for the cross classification of eighty-three occupational categories by four ethnic groups for two time periods. The saturated model is written as

$$F_{ijk} = \eta \; \tau_i^O \; \tau_j^E \; \tau_k^T \; \tau_{ij}^{OE} \; \tau_{ik}^{OT} \; \tau_{jk}^{ET} \; \tau_{ijk}^{OET}$$

where τ^O, τ^E, and τ^T are the main effects of occupation, ethnicity, and time respectively. τ^{OE}, τ^{OT}, and τ^{ET} are the effects of a two-way interaction, and τ^{OET} is the effect of a three-way interaction. The latter term is of particular interest because it represents the triple relationship among the three variables. It can be interpreted as measuring the extent to which the relationship between ethnicity and occupation changed over time (Hauser et al. 1975; Knoke and Burke 1980). A large coefficient would mean that the relationship was considerably altered; that is, the occupational distributions of ethnic groups changed in a dissimilar way and "pure" group mobility occurred. A coefficient negligible in size, however, would lead to the conclusion that the relationship between ethnicity and occupation remained stable over time and that, overall, ethnic groups were not occupationally mobile vis-à-vis one another.

Maximum likelihood estimates of the fit of several different models and the degrees of freedom associated with them are presented in table 3.2. In each model certain parameters are fixed, and the likelihood ratio statistics are then attributed to those relationships (described in the third column), which are free to vary. In model 1 only univariate marginals are fixed and the likelihood ratio ($L^2 = 23,198$) is attributable to the three two-way and one three-way relationships that are not fitted. Of the total 663 ($83 \times 4 \times 2 - 1 = 663$) degrees of freedom available in the table, 86 [$(83-1) + (4-1) + (2-1) = 86$] are used to fit model 1. Hence 577 degrees of freedom remain for testing the model. In contrast to model 1, in which all the parameters of the relationships are free to vary in fitting the data, model 5

TABLE 3.2 Loglinear Models for the Joint Distribution of Occupation, Ethnicity, and Time (male labor force)

Model	Marginals Fitted (1)	Model Description: Relationship Excluded (2)	L^2 (3)	Degrees of Freedom (4)	L^2/L_1^2 (5)	L^2/L_2^2 (6)
1	[occupation], [ethnicity] [time]	All relationships	23,198	577	—	—
2	[occupation, time] [ethnicity, time]	Ethnic stratification: 3-way interaction	18,367	492	—	—
3	[occupation, ethnicity] [occupation, time]	change: 3-way interaction	3303	249	.14	—
4	[occupation, ethnicity] [ethnicity, time]	Structural change: 3-way interaction	5080	328	.23	—
5	[occupation, ethnicity] [occupation, time] [ethnicity, time]	3-way interaction only	1030	246	.04	.05

controls for all relationships except the triple interaction. The likelihood ratio of the model ($L^2 = 1,030$), which is associated with 246 degrees of freedom, is uniquely attributable to the three-way interaction of occupation, ethnicity, and time.

A comparison of each of the models in table 3.2 and the saturated model (not shown because it has no degrees of freedom and $L^2 = 0.00$) indicates that in all cases estimates of the likelihood ratios are statistically significant ($\rho \leq 0.001$), which means that none of the models yields an acceptable overall fit to the data. The comparison of any pair of models in table 3.2, where the difference in L^2 relative to the difference in degrees of freedom associated with the models is taken as a statistical criterion for improvement in fitting the data (Upton 1978, 56), also yields significant results ($\rho \leq 0.001$). This finding is hardly surprising in view of the direct relationship between sample size and the magnitude of L^2. Because more than 50,000 cases were included in the analysis, just about any discrepancy between the observed and expected distributions would be statistically significant. Thus a more appropriate procedure for evaluating the substantive contribution of a given effect in large samples is to compute the reduction in L^2 associated with the model of interest relative to a base-line model (Goodman 1972; Knoke and Burke 1980; Stolzenberg and D'Amico 1977).

The model of independence (only main effects) is typically chosen as a base line for comparison. In the present case we are primarily interested in the magnitude of the unique three-way interaction, which, as noted earlier, is estimated in model 5. We therefore evaluate the likelihood ratio of model 5 as a proportion of the overall relationship among the variables, which is captured by model 1. The figure in the last row of column 5 (0.04 = 1030/23,198) indicates that only 4 percent of the variation in the base-line model might be attributed to the triple interaction. Indeed, change over time in the relationship between ethnicity and occupation only barely contributes to reproducing the observed distribution.

Because our central interest is the relationship between ethnicity and occupation, a more conservative model can be used as a base line for comparison. In model 2 the interaction between ethnicity and occupation is omitted, whereas the two-way relationships between occupation and time and ethnicity and time are fitted. The three-way relationship accounting for L^2 in model 5 is evaluated, then, as a proportion of the overall uncontrolled relationship between ethnicity and occupation (model 2). The result, presented in the bottom row of column 6, indicates that even with these assumptions the three-way interaction accounts for only 5 percent of the relationship. We can conclude, therefore, that although the relationship between ethnicity and occupation was altered somewhat between 1969 and 1982, the change accounted for only a minimal amount of the mobility that took place.

Using the same procedure of relative reduction in the likelihood ratio, it is possible to evaluate model 3 and model 4. The likelihood ratio associated with model 3 ($L^2 = 3303$) is attributable to the ethnicity–time relationship (and the three-way interaction), which is not fixed and which represents the change in ethnic composition. In model 4 the occupation–time interaction is free to fit the data, and the L^2 associated with the model is thus attributable to the structural change that took place. Both model 3 and model 4 are evaluated relative to the model of independence (model 1) to determine their contribution to the joint relationship between ethnicity, occupation, and time. The results, in the fifth column of table 3.2, indicate that the proportional contribution of compositional change estimated by model 3 is 0.14, compared with 0.23 in the case of model 4. The occupation–time interaction thus accounts for a larger proportion of the overall relationship than does the ethnicity–time interaction. Clearly, change in the occupational structure is central in determining the occupational distribution of ethnic groups over time.

Occupation-Specific Patterns of Ethnic Group Mobility

Up to this point we have been concerned with the placement of individuals from different ethnic backgrounds in the occupational system. We now shift our attention to a second, though related, issue: the extent of mobility, both in and out, characteristic of specific occupational categories. In addressing this issue, occupations rather than individuals are taken as units of analysis. When cast in these terms, the three-way interaction coefficients, extracted from the saturated loglinear model discussed earlier, may be used to characterize each occupation with regard to the extent of entry and exit of ethnic groups during the period of study. Although the triple interaction contributed little toward reproducing the occupational distribution of *individuals*, this does not necessarily mean that ethnic mobility across occupations did not take place. It simply indicates that its effect at the individual level was small relative to the overall variation among individuals (Fossett and Swicegood 1982). At the ecological level, however, deviations from the mean tendency may be of substantive interest in characterizing various occupations and in relating occupation-specific mobility to other occupational attributes.

Occupation-specific patterns of ethnic mobility, as indicated by the three-way interaction terms, can be more clearly assessed by means of odds ratios. The odds ratios are derived for each occupation from the cross classification of ethnicity (for pairs of ethnic groups) by time. The ratios are calculated as $(f_{11} \times f_{22}) / (f_{12} \times f_{21})$ where f_{11} is the number of individuals from ethnic group A employed in the occupation in 1969 and f_{12} is the number of members of group B in the occupation at the same point in time. f_{21} and f_{22} are the frequencies of the two groups, respectively, in 1982.[4] The greater the mobility of group A out of the occupation, the higher the ratio. These odds are directly related to the effect

---

4. Because odds for ratios that have zero in the denominator are undefined, a value of 0.001 is arbitrarily given in these cases.

of the three-way interaction in the saturated loglinear model and can be calculated as follows:

$$\frac{f_{i11}\,f_{i22}}{f_{i12}\,f_{i21}} = \left(\frac{\tau_{i11}^{OET}}{\tau_{i21}^{OET}}\right)^2 \times \left(\frac{\tau_{11}^{ET}}{\tau_{21}^{ET}}\right)^2$$

Because the second term on the right-hand side of the equation is constant for all occupational categories, the odds ratio and the three-way interaction term are perfectly correlated. The properties of the loglinear model ensure that confounding demographic or labor force processes are eliminated (Simpson et al. 1982). The odds ratios adjust for overall expansion of the labor force, growth or shrinkage of particular ethnic groups, and change in the size of the labor force of specific occupations.

Odds ratios were computed four times for the eighty-three occupations. Each time a different contrast for the two years (1969 and 1982) was specified. Contrasts were done for Jews (European-American and Asian-African combined) versus noncitizen Arabs;[5] Israeli Arabs versus noncitizen Arabs; Jews versus Israeli Arabs; and European-American Jews versus Asian-African Jews. These cross-product odds ratios were transformed to the logarithmic scale to modify the skew of the distribution and to minimize the possible effect of outliers. The means and standard deviations of the four distributions (across eighty-three occupations) were then calculated and are presented in the first two columns of table 3.3. The figures reveal differences among the contrasts as well as considerable variation among occupations within each contrast, as determined by the standard deviations. The mean scores for the first two contrasts indicate larger in-mobility of noncitizen Arabs relative to local ethnic groups. Differential mobility is less pronounced in contrasts of local ethnic groups (i.e., Jews versus Israeli Arabs and European-American Jews versus Asian-African Jews).

Considerable variation is found in the odds of mobility across occupations. Thus, although earlier findings indicate that the triple interaction played only a modest role in occupational distribution on the individual level, its consequences for changes over time at the occupational level were nonetheless important. In some

5. Separate analyses consistently showed identical patterns when the two Jewish groups were contrasted with Arabs. The two Jewish groups are thus combined in such contrasts in the remainder of the chapter.

TABLE 3.3 *Means, Standard Deviations (S.D.), and Percentile Positions of Logged Differential Odds of Mobility between 1969 and 1982 for Ethnic Contrasts in Eighty-three Occupational Categories and Illustrative Figures for Three Occupations*

			Percentiles[a]					Selected Occupations		
Contrasts	$\overline{X}$	S.D.	10	25	50	75	90	Office adminis-trators	Cooks and waiters	Unskilled laborers
Jews versus noncitizen Arabs	3.71	3.03	6.91[b]	6.91[b]	3.44	1.35	−.24	−1.74	1.01	2.66
Israeli Arabs versus noncitizen Arabs	3.41	3.34	6.91[b]	6.91[b]	3.29	1.11	−1.30	−0.43	−0.25	2.40
Jews versus Israeli Arabs	−0.12	0.76	.94	.33	.08	−.53	−1.15	−0.59	0.87	0.75
European-American versus Asian-African Jews	0.49	1.11	.99	.71	.29	.02	−.26	0.96	0.74	0.22

[a]Figures refer to the logged differential odds of mobility into or out of the occupation ranked at the given percentile point in the distribution.
[b]This figure was obtained for all occupations in which noncitizen Arabs were absent in 1969 (see note 4 in this chapter).

occupations the relative representation of the two groups did not change, resulting in ratios very close to a value of zero. In other occupations, the odds diverged considerably from unity, indicating different patterns of recruitment, retention of the two groups, or both (Simpson et al. 1982).

Both the standard deviation and percentile points reveal large differences in ethnic group mobility across occupations. In the first contrast, for example, the occupation at the fiftieth percentile experienced disproportionate in-mobility of Arabs or, alternatively, a large exit of Jews. This means that 50 percent of the occupations had a value larger than 3.44, indicating more intensive in-mobility of noncitizen Arabs overall. The odds of in-mobility to the occupation at the ninetieth percentile had a value of −0.24, that is, the odds of entering the occupation were 1.27 to 1.00 in favor of Jews. This pattern of differential mobility was not unique to the first contrast. A look at the odds ratios for other pairs of ethnic groups confirms that in all cases considerable variation existed in ethnic group mobility in and out of occupations between 1969 and 1982.

To help in understanding the interpretation of differential mobility in the present context, the logged odds ratios for three occupations are presented for illustrative purposes. Negative values indicate larger relative in-mobility of the group listed first in the contrast, whereas positive values indicate the opposite. Values close to zero mean that in- or out-mobility of the two ethnic groups was similar. In the case of office administrators there was greater in-mobility for Jews when they were compared separately to noncitizen Arabs and to Israeli Arabs (−1.74 and −0.59 respectively). Mobility of Israeli Arabs into this occupation was somewhat higher than that of noncitizen Arabs, as indicated by the odds ratio of −0.43. Among Jews, the entry of Asian-Africans exceeded that of European-Americans. Somewhat different patterns were revealed by the other occupations. Jews tended to exit the occupational category of cooks and waiters, whereas Israeli Arabs experienced the largest in-mobility. Finally, in the case of unskilled labor, Jews and Israeli Arabs had higher out-mobility rates than did noncitizen Arabs. The exit of Jews, however, was more pronounced than that of Israeli Arabs (odds ratio of 0.75), and within the Jewish population European-Americans were more likely to exit the occupation than were Asian-Africans.

Determinants of Occupation-Specific Ethnic Group Mobility

The sociological literature cited at the outset of this chapter led us to anticipate that differential group mobility would be systematically related to occupational characteristics. In particular, we expected that differential mobility, expressed in the odds ratios, would be related to the socioeconomic status of an occupation and penetration of the subordinate ethnic group. Regression models were therefore examined to contrast the differential mobility of the four ethnic groups. In each model, differential group mobility, measured by the cross-product odds ratios, was taken as a function of occupational SES, growth of noncitizen Arabs, and proportion of wage earners in the occupation. The latter was added as a control variable.[6] Standardized regression coefficients estimated for these models are presented in table 3.4.

The differential mobility of Jews versus noncitizen Arabs is shown in model 1. The statistically significant negative coefficient of SES ($\beta = -0.26$) indicates that the higher the status of an occupation, the greater the likelihood of Jewish in-mobility relative to in-mobility of noncitizen Arabs.[7] In other words, Jews were not only higher in the occupational hierarchy between 1969 and 1982 but upwardly mobile relative to the subordinate group. In 1969, the proportion of noncitizen Arabs in an occupation was negatively related to the dependent variable even when SES was controlled.

At first sight this finding seems somewhat curious. It suggests that the higher the proportion of Arabs from the administered territories in an occupation, the greater the likelihood that Jews would enter the occupation. The more appropriate interpretation, however, appears to be that the *lower* the proportion of Arabs from the administered territories in an occupation at the initial point in time, the greater their mobility (relative to that of Jews) into the occupation. This explanation supports the finding that there was profound penetration of Arabs from the territories throughout the occupational structure during the period. Finally, the negative

6. Other variables that were considered were the mean age and unemployment rate in the occupation. These variables did not improve upon previous models, however, and for the sake of parsimony are not reported.

7. Alternatively, one may conclude that the lower the status, the greater the out-mobility of Jews and the greater the in-mobility of noncitizen Arabs.

TABLE 3.4 Standardized Regression Coefficients for Models Predicting the Odds of Differential Mobility between 1969 and 1982 for Ethnic Contrasts in Eighty-three Occupational Categories (standard errors in parentheses)

	Group Mobility (ln odds) 1969–82			
Independent Variables	*Jews vs. Arabs from Territories* (1)	*Israeli Arabs vs. Arabs from Territories* (2)	*Jews vs. Israeli Arabs* (3)	*European-American vs. Asian-African Jews* (4)
SES of occupation	−.26 (.10)	−.29 (.11)	−.35 (.12)	.16 (.14)
Proportion of noncitizen Arabs, 1969[a]	−47 (.10)	−.39 (.10)		
Change in proportion of noncitizen Arabs, 1969–82			.16 (.09)	.04 (.12)
Proportion of wage earners in occupation	.28 (.09)	.26 (.10)	−.09 (.10)	−.11 (.11)
R^2	.31	.27	.22	.03

[a]Proportion rather than change in proportion was used in the first two models because change in proportion is itself an indicator of mobility for noncitizen Arabs.

coefficient for the effect of proportion of wage earners indicates that, controlling for the previous two variables, the higher the proportion of wage earners in the occupation, the greater the likelihood that noncitizen Arabs would enter. As expected, members of the subordinate group were barred from occupations that had opportunities for self-employment and entrepreneurship and were relegated to wage-earning jobs.

Model 2 in table 3.4 compares the mobility of Israeli Arabs with that of noncitizen Arabs. As in the previous case, the coefficients for SES and for the proportion of noncitizen Arabs are negative and the coefficient for proportion salaried in the occupation is positive. Apparently the social mechanisms that operated to distinguish mobility of Jews from that of noncitizen Arabs were essentially similar in the case of Israeli Arabs.[8]

Both Jews and Israeli Arabs enjoyed upward mobility relative to the subordinate group of "newcomers." It is not clear, however, to what extent endogenous groups experienced differential mobility vis-à-vis one another and how such mobility was related to the socioeconomic standing of an occupation and to the entry of noncitizen Arabs into the occupation. Thus in model 3 a regression coefficient is estimated predicting differential mobility of Jews versus Israeli Arabs, whereas model 4 contrasts the two Jewish groups.

The most significant effect observed in model 3 is that of occupational SES, indicating that the higher the status of the occupation, the greater the likelihood of in-mobility of Jews relative to Israeli Arabs. Although both groups were upwardly mobile, the superordinate group of Jews "did better" than Israeli Arabs

---

8. The coefficients presented in table 3.4 provide a conservative estimate of the effect of SES on relative in- and out-mobility because we made the assumption in constructing the dependent variable that there was no mobility for occupations in which noncitizen Arabs were not present in 1969 (this was done so that odds ratios would not have zeros in the denominator). When we relax this assumption and include occupations that grew from zero noncitizen Arabs (0.5 was the number used) to some positive number, the standardized equations obtained are as follows:

Group mobility of Jews versus noncitizen Arabs $= -0.59 \times$ SES $-0.35 \times$ proportion of noncitizen Arabs in 1969 $+ 0.23 \times$ proportion of wage earners in the occupation $(R^2 = 0.39)$

Group mobility of Israeli Arabs versus noncitizen Arabs $= -0.54 \times$ SES $- 0.22 \times$ proportion of noncitizen Arabs in 1969 $+ 0.18 \times$ proportion of wage earners in the occupation $(R^2 = 0.29)$

and were able to seize more preferred opportunities. Entry of Arabs from the administered territories had some effect, though not statistically significant, on the differential mobility of Jews and Israeli Arabs. The more rapid the increase in the number of new-comers in an occupation, the greater the out-mobility of Jews relative to Arabs. Such a process means that certain occupations were becoming "more Arab" in their composition, even within socioeconomic categories.

In the last contrast, shown in model 4, none of the coefficients was significantly different from zero. The reader should recall that data on table 3.3 indicated that the two Jewish groups experienced considerable differential mobility across occupations. Even so, when mobility took place, it was not systematically related to any of the variables included in the model. In other words, the two groups were not differentially affected by either the entry of non-citizen Arabs or the status of the occupation. The two Jewish groups retained their *relative* hierarchical position in the occupational structure.

Interpreting Ethnic Group Mobility

The analysis in this chapter provides several important insights concerning stratification and mobility in multiethnic societies. Before turning to the theoretical concerns that guided the analysis, a number of specific findings regarding Israeli society will be recounted. During the period under study, all three endogenous ethnic groups in Israel improved their socioeconomic positions. Nevertheless, as evident from the loglinear analysis, the *relationship* between ethnicity and occupation was barely altered during the period, despite the large influx of noncitizen Arabs. In fact, changes in the ethnic composition of the work force were of secondary importance in determining the observed occupational distributions. The variable that most affected individual occupational mobility was structural shift, which brought about a considerable upgrading in the occupational system.

Although compositional changes had only a slight effect on overall mobility, further analysis showed considerable variability in occupation-specific patterns of in- and out-mobility. Between 1969 and 1982 endogenous ethnic groups, both Jews and Arabs, entered higher-status occupations and vacated those in which in-mobility of noncitizen Arabs took place. A comparison of the mobility of Jews and of Israeli Arabs further indicated that the gap between Jews and Arabs was growing. Although both groups were mobile, Jews were more successful in entering advantageous positions in the occupational hierarchy. Jews also tended more rapidly to leave occupations in which the number of noncitizen Arabs was growing disproportionately, thus leading to more pronounced ethnic differentiation. Within the Jewish population occupational mobility was not related either to status or to growth of the subordinate group. Thus, although Asian-African Jews were upwardly mobile, neither entry of noncitizen Arabs into the labor market nor the structural changes that took place altered their occupational standing vis-à-vis European-American Jews.

Taken as a whole, the findings highlight the dynamics of ethnic changes in Israel. European-American and Asian-African Jews were equally likely to improve their occupational status. Thus the relative gap between the groups remained stable over time. Arabs, in contrast, could not fully take advantage of the occupational opportunities made available. Although Israeli Arabs enjoyed some upward mobility, the gap between them and Jews grew wider. The influx of noncitizen Arabs to certain occupations, combined with the rapid exit of Jews, upheld the caste line in the occupational system. Arabs must not be viewed as a single entity, however. Indeed, the differential mobility of Israeli Arabs and noncitizen Arabs underscores that the latter group participates in the Israeli economy under the most disadvantageous circumstances. Lacking political power, citizenship rights, and feasible economic alternatives, they are destined to occupy only those positions shunned by other groups. They entered at the bottom of the occupational ladder in 1969 and remained there during a time when all other groups benefited from structural mobility.

Queuing and overflow models of ethnic stratification center on the effect of change in ethnic composition on a group's occupational mobility. Our findings lend firm support to these theses. Rapid growth of the subordinate ethnic group was related to upward mobility of all groups higher in the ethnic hierarchy. Furthermore, when more than one group stood to benefit from entry and growth of the subordinate group, those at the top benefited more from the change in ethnic composition. One shortcoming of previous work on ethnic stratification has been its failure to incorporate explicitly structural changes into models of ethnic group mobility. The findings reported here have a direct bearing on this issue insofar as structural change proved to be a more important determinant of the occupational mobility of ethnic groups than compositional change. Evidently, the queuing and overflow models underestimate the extent of differential mobility and the advantages enjoyed by superordinate ethnic groups.

4
Occupational Segregation and Income Competition

The data presented thus far indicate rather clearly that noncitizen Arabs are concentrated at the lowest rungs of the occupational ladder and are absent from socially and economically rewarding occupations. Indeed, exclusionary processes have been observed by virtually all students of economic discrimination to have detrimental consequences for the income of subordinate ethnic groups. Ethnic minorities are denied access to the lucrative and prestigious occupations and are thus relegated to the low-paying jobs. At the core of these processes is the Weberian notion of "closure"—"the process by which social collectivities seek to maximize rewards by restricting access to resources and opportunities to a limited circle of eligibles" (Parkin 1979, 44).

Although the literature on the causes and consequences of exclusion is substantial, only a few studies have examined its impact on the income of superordinates. One group of studies has examined whether superordinates gain or lose by practicing labor market discrimination (Beck 1980; Glenn 1963; Reich 1971; Szymanski 1976; Villemez 1978). Another body of research has focused on whether changes in the levels of occupational segregation affect the income level of superordinates (Hodge and Hodge 1965 and 1966; Snyder and Hudis 1976; Taeuber et al. 1966). This latter body of literature—presenting what are known as the competition versus segregation hypotheses—is mainly concerned with the causal mechanism underlying the dynamics of occupational segregation and its relationship to income. More specifically, it focuses on the question of whether entry of an ethnic minority into an occupational labor market has detrimental consequences for the income of superordinates.

In this chapter we examine the extent to which the incorporation of Arabs into lower-status occupations resulted in the deterioration of the income levels of Jews and Israeli Arabs employed in these occupations. The analysis is carried out within the framework of the competition versus segregation debate. We will first seek to clarify the meaning of competition and segregation in modern economies and the conditions under which they arise. Second, we will detail the interrelations between these two social processes. Finally, we will discuss the findings in light of the theoretical notion of exclusion.

Theoretical Models of Competition and Segregation

Sociologists have long been concerned with the relationship between the composition of a labor market and income discrimination. They uniformly agree that occupational labor markets are segregated along racial lines and have repeatedly demonstrated that an influx of minority group members into the labor force is likely to result in greater occupational differentiation (Frisbie and Neidert 1977; Lieberson 1980; Semyonov et al. 1984; Fossett 1984). Consequently, both sociologists and economists have focused on the mechanisms by which economic discrimination prevails. The explanations that have been proposed include formulations emphasizing human capital, overcrowding, statistical discrimination, and labor market structure.

Although the literature on the significance of structural characteristics of occupational labor markets in determining wage differentials has grown rapidly in recent years (e.g., Stolzenberg 1975a and 1975b; Spilerman 1977; Hudson and Kaufman 1982; Kaufman 1983), the competition-segregation debate has received less than appropriate attention. The neglect is unfortunate in that the debate has general theoretical implications for research on segmented labor markets, dual economies, and split labor markets.

Students of occupational labor markets have advanced two explanations regarding the relationship between the composition of the labor force and income discrimination. The two approaches emphasized in the literature are labeled the competition and the segregation hypotheses (Snyder and Hudis 1976). Hodge and

Hodge (1965 and 1966) proposed the competition hypothesis, according to which entrance of subordinate groups into the labor force of an occupation depresses the income level of incumbents in the occupation. In contrast, Taeuber et al. (1966) advocated the segregation hypothesis, which suggests that better-paying occupations deny access to subordinate ethnic groups. Snyder and Hudis (1976) take issue with both these positions and conclude that neither competition nor segregation is empirically significant; if anything, competition and segregation are sex- and race-specific. Competition operates in the case of gender, whereas segregation appears to operate in the case of race.

The competition hypothesis is derived from the marginal productivity model and focuses on the differential ability of individual workers or groups to compete in the labor market. Proponents of this approach (Hodge and Hodge 1965 and 1966) assert that perfect competition in the labor market does not exist and that the wages of certain groups of workers are determined not only by their productivity but by the composition (sex or race) of the labor market in which they are employed. In fact, they say racial and gender discrimination alters the nature of competition in occupations in which a substantial proportion of the employees are minorities. As proponents of this view, the Hodges argue that the entrance of minority workers into an occupation engenders competition with superordinates in that the former, because of discrimination, are "willing" to work for lower wages. They contend that "some groups find the conditions of work less negotiable than others. . . . When such groups supply their labor at a lower cost, they may well lead to the deterioration of the working conditions enjoyed by other groups" (1965, 250). According to the competition view, the entrance of subordinate groups into the labor force of an occupation affects the wage structure by depressing the income of superordinates.

By contrast, the segregation hypothesis suggests that better-paying occupations use barriers such as unions, licensing requirements, and specific job prerequisites to exclude subordinate groups. Minority workers are thus systematically denied access to lucrative and prestigious occupations and are segregated to undesirable jobs. Proponents of the segregation hypothesis (Taeuber et al. 1966) imply that there should be perfect competition among individuals or social groups within occupations and that the social composition of the labor force of an occupation should not affect wage differentials between groups. (Hodge and Hodge [1966] comment on this issue.) According to this hypothesis, then, the key to explaining income discrimination lies in processes that deny individuals access to occupations rather than in processes taking place within the occupations.

Hodge and Hodge (1965) and Taeuber et al. (1966) have relied mainly on cross-sectional data. Stemming from different theoretical orientations, each interpreted the negative relationship between ethnic composition and income (even when controlling for other variables) as lending support for their arguments. Both groups of researchers acknowledged, of course, the difficulty of ascertaining causal direction from cross-sectional analysis. They therefore supplemented their analysis with longitudinal, though partial, data to estimate change over time.[1] Nevertheless, a different model was specified in each analysis. Hodge and Hodge tested a model in which change in income was the dependent variable and ethnic composition at the initial point in time was the independent variable. Taeuber et al. tested a model in which change in composition was dependent and income at the initial point in time was the determinant. Both groups found confirmation for their theoretical propositions, but it is not clear whether their different conclusions were a result of their different theoretical positions, different methods of measurement, or both.

Snyder and Hudis (1976) have argued, and justifiably so, that the causal direction could be ascertained with greater confidence using a two-wave, two-variable model within the framework of path analysis (Heise 1970; Kessler and Greenberg 1981). The basic model was quite straightforward and has been described at length by Snyder and Hudis (1976). Figure 4.1 provides a schematic presentation of the model. According to the figure, the paths $I_2 I_1$ and $P_2 P_1$ represent stability in the income structure and ethnic composition of occupations, respectively. The path $P_2 I_1$ represents the effect of income structure on the change in ethnic composition, and the path $I_2 P_1$ stands for the effect of ethnic composition on change in the income level. The path $e_I e_P$ rep-

---

1. These analyses were performed on a limited number of operative occupations for which data were available at two points in time. Data for a more detailed set of occupations did not exist at that time.

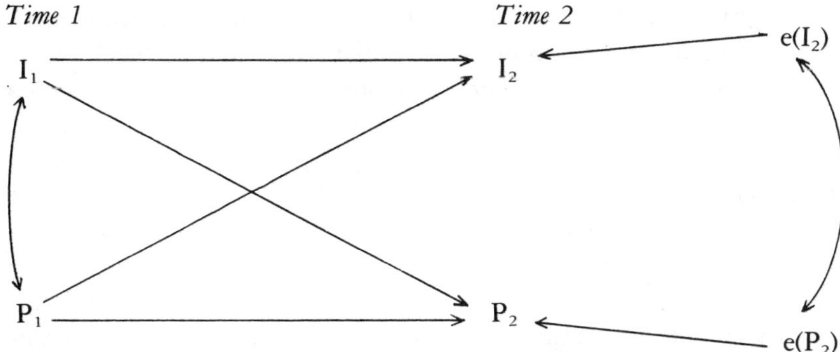

I = income of dominant group; P = proportion of minority group; e = disturbance term.

FIGURE 4.1 *Two-Wave, Two-Variable Model Representing Competition and Segregation*

resents the correlation between the two residual terms, that is, the correlation between the remaining unexplained variation in income and in ethnic composition.

According to Snyder and Hudis, if the segregation hypothesis prevailed one would have expected a negative direct effect of income level at the initial point in time on the proportion of subordinates in the occupation at a later point in time (P_2 I_1). In contrast, a negative direct effect of proportion of subordinates at the initial point in time on income level of superordinates at the later time was taken as support for the competition hypothesis (I_2 P_1). Indeed, in both cases the direct effects represented the impact of either income level or proportion of subordinates on *change* in the alternate variable.[2]

Surprisingly, Snyder and Hudis have not provided (or at least did not report) an estimate of the correlation between the residuals in the model (e_I e_P). We cannot conceive of either a theoretical or an empirical reason to assume that the error terms in the model are uncorrelated. Furthermore, the correlation between the errors

2. It is important to emphasize that the model entailed certain assumptions, the most important of which was that there were no instantaneous effects and that the lag period approximated the measurement period. For a more detailed discussion of this topic, see Snyder and Hudis (1976), pp. 219–20.

can be interpreted as meaning that there was simultaneous change in the proportion of subordinates and in the income level of the occupation (Bohrnstedt 1969; Semyonov and Scott 1983). Such a relationship, though unnecessary for the segregation hypothesis, has been explicitly advocated by proponents of the competition model (Hodge and Hodge 1965 and 1966).

From a statistical point of view it is impossible, of course, to determine the causal relationship between the residual terms in the model. Our argument on this matter, however, is theoretical. From a theoretical point of view the two models involve different perceptions of the labor market. The segregation hypothesis proposes that income discrimination is regulated by "sorting" mechanisms. Higher-paying occupations establish effective barriers to exclude members of subordinate ethnic groups. Within occupations, however, individuals are paid equitably without regard to their ethnic origin. Thus, once one controls for the lagged effect of income on percentage of minority workers, there is no reason, according to this hypothesis, to expect a simultaneous decline in income and in the proportion of minority workers in the occupation. The competition model, by contrast, assumes a market situation in which wage competition takes place, that is, the composition of the labor force of an occupation determines wage differentials and alters labor market competition. Thus, as the number of workers from the subordinate group increases, superordinates face more severe competition and consequently suffer a decline in income. According to this view, the process of change in composition and in income occurs simultaneously. Thus, whereas segregation can be evaluated by means of the lagged effect of income on composition, competition is more properly estimated by the correlation between the residuals.[3]

In this chapter we argue that neither perfect segregation nor perfect competition exist in modern labor markets. Thus the de-

---

3. Although our theoretical model suggests that the correlated residual terms in the analytical model imply simultaneous change in income and composition, there may of course be other statistical reasons and alternative explanations for why the error terms are correlated. There may be no simultaneous effects but common unmeasured causes of income and composition that were not included in the model or no simultaneous effects but correlated measurement errors. Although we have no way of choosing here between explanations, it should be noted that we are actually testing the hypothesis that correlated errors simply imply simultaneous change. This hypothesis was derived from the theoretical reasoning discussed at the outset of the chapter.

TABLE 4.1 *Income Ranking of Selected Occupational Categories in 1969, 1975, and 1981 (1 = highest, 83 = lowest)*

Occupational Category	1969	1975	1981
Pharmacists	20	13	19
Engineers	11	6	7
Bookkeepers and cashiers	19	21	23
Retail tradesmen	66	59	69
Electricians	33	26	30
Construction workers	31	29	49
Dyers	45	50	56
Road construction workers	27	33	63
Cooks and waiters	56	44	76
Porters	63	56	66
Painters	71	53	74
Unskilled laborers	79	69	82
Tailors	59	66	75

gree of competition is dependent on the existence of some degree of segregation. Nonetheless, segregation is by no means a sufficient condition for the emergence of "competition discrimination." Group strength and the social and political context may also emerge as significant determinants of competition.

Occupational Income and Noncitizen Arabs

The analysis thus far has underscored rather clearly that noncitizen Arabs were concentrated at the bottom of the occupational ladder. Furthermore, the data indicated that their concentration in lower-status occupations increased, rather than decreased, over the years. The extent to which the employment of noncitizen Arabs in lower-status occupations had a detrimental effect on the income levels of other incumbents in these occupations will be examined in this chapter.

Before turning to a systematic and rigorous analysis of this issue we will first demonstrate for a select number of occupations the relationship between the income level of an occupation and the percentage of noncitizen Arabs employed. Thirteen occupational categories are presented in table 4.1. Each occupation was given its relative rank-order position with regard to the mean income level of Israeli male employees. In 1969, for example, engineers were ranked 11 with respect to income, whereas unskilled laborers were ranked 79 (based on eighty-three occupational categories). In 1981, engineers were ranked 7, whereas unskilled laborers were ranked 82. Hence a comparison across the columns of table 4.1 enables us to evaluate changes in the position of each occupation relative to other occupations during the period under study.[4]

The occupations listed in table 4.1 represent two distinct groups: (1) occupations from which noncitizen Arabs were absent, presented at the top of the table, which include pharmacists, engineers, bookkeepers, and electricians; and (2) occupations that gained a disproportionately large number of noncitizen Arab workers during the period, including construction workers, road construction workers, cooks, waiters, tailors, and unskilled laborers.

Two major conclusions are readily apparent from the data presented in table 4.1. First, occupations from which noncitizen Arabs were absent were characterized by higher income levels. Second, considerable change occurred in the relative position of occupations with regard to income level. These changes were generally related to a change in the number of noncitizen Arab employees. It is apparent that occupations that experienced a large influx of noncitizen Arab workers also experienced a decline in their income rankings. The changes were especially pronounced in the case of construction and road construction workers. The ranking of the latter category dropped from 27 in 1969 to 33 in 1975 and plummeted further to 63 (out of 83) by 1981. The decline was less pronounced in the case of unskilled laborers, probably because of a "floor effect." Unskilled laborers were already practically at the bottom of the income ranking in 1969, so there was very little room for further decline. In contrast, the position of occupations in which noncitizen Arabs did not enter remained relatively stable throughout the period: the position of electricians improved from a rank of 33 to 30, whereas that of engineers climbed from 11 to 7. The position of bookkeepers declined some-

---

4. Relative ranking was preferred over absolute figures because high levels of inflation and a change in the Israeli currency during the period rendered a comparison over time particularly cumbersome.

what, and the position of pharmacists remained virtually unchanged.

The few cases displayed in table 4.1 were chosen for illustrative purposes. By no means do they represent the entire range of occupational categories. Nonetheless, they demonstrate a clear and meaningful association between income levels and participation of noncitizen Arabs in occupational domains. The causal direction of the relationship, however, is not evident from the findings reported thus far. It is not clear whether the increase in participation of noncitizen Arabs led to the deterioration of the income of other incumbents in the occupation or whether noncitizen Arabs were "permitted" to join occupations in which income levels were declining. In the analysis that follows we will use more systematic and rigorous methods to address these questions.

Noncitizen Arabs and Income of Israeli Workers

Analysis was performed on the eighty-three occupational categories within the framework of the two-wave, two-variable regression model.[5] Lagged effects as well as the correlation between the residuals were estimated. We began by estimating coefficients of the model for the period 1969–81. Both the ethnic composition and the income level of the occupation were measured in 1969 (the initial point in time) and in 1981 (the later point in time). These two variables are central to the theoretical models outlined at the outset of the chapter. Ethnic composition of each occupation was defined as the percentage of noncitizen male Arabs (PNCA) who found employment in the occupation. Income level was measured for salaried Israeli male workers (LNINC) in the occupation. Coefficients for the simultaneous equations for the two-wave, two-variable model are presented in columns 1 and 2 of table 4.2. Models that included additional control variables appear in columns 3 and 4 of the same table. These additional variables, measured at the initial point in time, are AGE—the average age of male workers in the occupation; SAL—percentage of salaried work-

5. A more detailed classification of occupations was available for the period 1975–81, permitting an analysis of eighty-seven occupational categories. The results of this analysis did not differ substantially, however, from those obtained for the original eighty-three categories.

TABLE 4.2. Estimates of Basic Two-Wave and Extended Two-Wave Path Models (standard errors in parentheses) Predicting Income of Israeli Workers (LNINC) and Percentage of Noncitizen Arabs (PNCA) in Eighty-three Occupational Categories, 1969–81

Independent Variables (at initial time)[a]	Basic Model		Extended Model	
	PNCA, 1981	LNINC, 1981	PNCA, 1981	LNINC, 1981
LNINC, 1969	$-.19^b$	$.74^b$	$-.18^c$	$.65^b$
	(.10)	(.08)	(.11)	(.08)
PNCA, 1969	$.53^b$	$-.11$	$.50^b$	$-.06$
	(.10)	(.08)	(.10)	(.07)
AGE, 1969	—	—	.09	$-.15^c$
			(.11)	(.08)
UNR, 1969	—	—	.13	$-.28$
			(.11)	(.08)
SAL, 1969	—	—	.09	.04
			(.10)	(.08)
Correlation between residuals	$-.27^b$		$-.29^b$	
R^2	.37	.59	.39	.66

[a]See text for definitions of variables.
[b]$p \leq .05$.
[c]$p \leq .10$.

ers in the occupation; and UNR—percentage unemployed in the occupation.

The results for the basic model (columns 1 and 2) were essentially similar to those obtained for the extended model (columns 3 and 4). Noncitizen Arabs tended to find employment in occupations in which income was relatively low. The stability factors in both the income level and ethnic structures of occupations were substantial. That is, occupations tended to maintain their relative hierarchical positions during the period under investigation. Nevertheless, stability coefficients were considerably lower than 1.0, indicating some looseness in the structure and extensive change in both the income level and ethnic composition of the occupation. The percentage of noncitizen Arabs had virtually no effect on the income of Israeli workers. Income level had a significant negative effect on the percentage of noncitizen Arabs in the occupation. Curiously, however, the most significant relationship was that observed between the two residual terms. The negative correlation clearly indicates that occupations that experienced disproportionate growth in the number of noncitizen Arabs were characterized by a disproportionate decline in the income level of Israeli workers. The dynamic relationship between composition and income is best understood as a process of interrelated simultaneous changes. Apparently noncitizen Arabs were disproportionately channeled into low-income occupations. Their influx into these labor markets generated greater competition, which, in turn, depressed the income of Israeli incumbents.

The models presented in table 4.2 provide estimates of the process of change for the period from 1969 to 1981. This time span, however, can be divided into two distinct intervals. The first interval, 1969–75, was characterized by dramatic growth in the number of noncitizen Arabs who joined the Israeli economy. During this period their number rose from approximately 9,000 to 65,000. In 1969, they accounted for only 1 percent of the male labor force; by 1975, they represented 6 percent. The 1975–81 interval was characterized by a moderate increase in the number of noncitizen Arab workers, and by the end of the period, approximately 75,000 had joined the economy. Because the two intervals are considerably different, it is essential to examine whether the findings in table 4.2 reflect processes that took place in only one of the periods and not the other.

The models were reestimated for each of the two periods, and the findings are presented in table 4.3. In all models the residual terms were negatively correlated, thus reaffirming the basic conclusions reached earlier. Regardless of the time period, a disproportionate increase in the number of noncitizen Arabs who entered an occupation was significantly related to a simultaneous decline in the income of Israeli workers who remained in the occupation. The effect of income level on change in the percentage of noncitizen Arabs (segregation) was considerably different in the two periods. Occupational segregation was more intensive in the earlier period. This finding is consistent with the extensive literature that demonstrates that a rapid increase in the size of a minority population results in greater occupational segregation (e.g., Broom and Glenn 1965; Martin and Poston 1972; Frisbie and Neidert 1977; Fossett 1984). Not only were noncitizen Arabs increasingly segregated to low-income occupations but their entrance to an occupational labor market apparently had detrimental consequences for the income of other incumbents.

TABLE 4.3 *Estimates of Extended Two-Wave Path Models (standard errors in parentheses) Predicting Income of Israeli Workers (LNINC) and Percentage of Noncitizen Arabs (PNCA) for 1969–75 and 1975–81 Periods in Eighty-three Occupational Categories*

	1969–75		1975–81	
Independent Variables (at initial time)[a]	PNCA, 1975 (1)	LNINC, 1975 (2)	PNCA, 1981 (3)	LNINC, 1981 (4)
LNINC	−.26[b]	.48[b]	−.02	.53[b]
	(.10)	(.11)	(.08)	(.10)
PNCA	.51[b]	−.09	.70[b]	−.04
	(.09)	(.10)	(.08)	(.10)
AGE	.02	−.08	.05	−.16[c]
	(.10)	(.11)	(.07)	(.09)
UNR	.07	−.11	.08	−.16[c]
	(.10)	(.11)	(.07)	(.09)
SAL	.19[c]	.19[c]	−.17[b]	.11
	(.10)	(.10)	(.08)	(.10)
Correlation between residuals	−.28[b]		−.30[b]	
R^2	.45	.39	.65	.46

[a]See text for definitions of variables.
[b]$p \leq .05$.
[c]$p \leq .10$.

Noncitizen Arabs and Income of Jewish Workers

Israel is far from a homogeneous society. Its population includes a large Arab minority (about 17 percent) who have been citizens of Israel since the establishment of the state in 1948. Although Israeli Arabs enjoy citizenship rights, they are subordinate to the Jewish population in all aspects of socioeconomic status (Peres 1971; Simon 1978; Semyonov and Tyree 1981). Israeli Arabs are more traditional than the Jewish population, and most live in villages and small towns. Noncitizen Arabs who joined the Israeli economy after 1967 tended to enter occupations in which Israeli Arabs were concentrated. Thus, to the degree that occupational integration generated competition, it is plausible to expect that the entry of noncitizen Arabs would be more detrimental to the income of Israeli Arabs than to the income of Jews.

Unfortunately, we were unable to examine this hypothesis directly because of the small number of occupations for which the income of Israeli Arabs could be estimated. We could, however, estimate the effect the employment of noncitizen Arabs had on the income of Jews. In addition, the findings for the total population enabled us to make inferences about the interrelationship between change in the percentage of noncitizen Arabs and income of Israeli Arabs.

Table 4.4 includes three models relating the income of Jews to the percentage of noncitizen Arabs in an occupation. The model for the entire period (1969–81) is presented in columns 1 and 2, the model for the period 1969–75 in columns 3 and 4, and the model for the years 1975–81 in columns 5 and 6. The findings revealed by all three models lead to the same basic conclusions arrived at for the total Israeli labor force (tables 4.1 and 4.2). The income of Jewish incumbents in an occupation had a negative effect on the percentage of noncitizen Arabs who entered the occupation. That is, noncitizen Arabs were denied access to the more lucrative jobs. In conjunction with occupational segregation, the two residual terms in all three models are negatively correlated. These negative correlations indicate that occupations that experienced unusual growth in the participation of noncitizen Arabs were also characterized by simultaneous decline in the income of Jewish workers. The entrance of noncitizen Arabs into an occupational labor force was detrimental to the income of Jewish workers who remained in the occupation. A comparison of the findings in table 4.4 and previous findings suggests that the income of both Jews and Israeli Arabs was similarly related to the entry of noncitizen Arabs into occupational labor markets.

Israeli Arabs and Income of Jewish Workers

At this point in the analysis we wish to explore whether the causal dynamics underlying labor force composition and income of superordinates observed in the case of noncitizen Arabs are general in nature and function for other subordinate groups. Because Israeli Arabs have citizenship rights and benefit from union protection and such labor legislation as equal pay and minimum wage, it is doubtful that wage competition similar to that observed from noncitizen Arabs would operate in the case of Israeli Arabs. Thus, in table 4.5, models are presented in which the percentage of Israeli Arabs in the occupation is substituted for the percentage of noncitizen Arabs.

TABLE 4.4 *Estimates of Extended Two-Wave Path Models (standard errors in parentheses) Predicting Income of Jewish Workers (LNJINC) and Percentage of Noncitizen Arabs (PNCA) for 1969–81, 1969–75, and 1975–81 in Eighty-three Occupational Categories*

Independent Variables (at initial time)[a]	1969–81		1969–75		1975–81	
	PNCA (1)	LNJINC (2)	PNCA (3)	LNJINC (4)	PNCA (5)	LNJINC (6)
LNJINC	$-.17^c$	$.61^b$	$-.26^b$	$.41^b$	$-.04$	$.54^b$
	(.10)	(.09)	(.10)	(.11)	(.08)	(.10)
PNCA	$.50^b$	$-.05$	$.51^b$	$-.01$	$.72^b$	$-.04$
	(.10)	(.08)	(.09)	(.10)	(.08)	(.10)
AGE	.09	$-.17$	.02	$-.14$	.05	$-.17^c$
	(.11)	(.09)	(.10)	(.11)	(.07)	(.09)
UNR	.13	$-.26^b$	.07	$-.16$	.11	$-.15$
	(.11)	(.09)	(.10)	(.11)	(.07)	(.09)
SAL	.09	.08	$.19^c$	$.18^c$	$-.09$	.10
	(.10)	(.08)	(.10)	(.11)	(.08)	(.10)
Correlation between residuals	$-.15^c$		$-.20^b$		$-.32^b$	
R^2	.38	.60	.45	.31	.64	.47

[a]See text for definitions of variables.
[b]$p \leq .5$.
[c]$p \leq .10$.

TABLE 4.5 *Estimates of Extended Two-Wave Path Models (standard errors in parentheses) Predicting Income of Jewish Workers (LNJINC) and Percentage of Israeli Arabs (PISA) for 1969–81, 1969–75, and 1975–81 in Eighty-three Occupational Categories*

Independent Variables (at initial time)[a]	1969–81		1969–75		1975–81	
	PISA (1)	LNJINC (2)	PISA (3)	LNJINC (4)	PISA (5)	LNJINC (6)
LNJINC	−.32[b]	.60[b]	−.28[b]	.40[b]	−.10	.55[b]
	(.11)	(.09)	(.09)	(.11)	(.07)	(.10)
PISA	.34[b]	−.06	.57[b]	−.05	.92[b]	−.10
	(.10)	(.08)	(.08)	(.11)	(.07)	(.10)
AGE	−.07	−.18[b]	−.21[b]	−.14	.07	−.25[b]
	(.11)	(.09)	(.09)	(.11)	(.06)	(.09)
UNR	.05	−.27[b]	−.08	−.15	−.01	.07
	(.11)	(.09)	(.09)	(.11)	(.06)	(.09)
SAL	−.05	.07	−.10	.18	.09	−.00
	(.10)	(.08)	(.08)	(.11)	(.07)	(.11)
Correlation between residuals	.03		.16[c]		.01	
R^2	.35	.60	.57	.31	.74	.42

[a]See text for definitions of variables.
[b]$p \leq .05$.
[c]$p \leq .10$.

Israeli Arabs generally found employment in occupations in which the income of Jews was comparatively low. When the occupational structure of Israeli Arabs at the initial point in time was taken into account, it became apparent that they were increasingly denied access to lucrative occupations. The cross-lagged effect of income level on change in the percentage of Israeli Arabs in the occupation was negative. This process of segregation was somewhat less pronounced during the latter period. The cross-lagged effect of percentage of Israeli Arabs on change in income level was insignificant. Furthermore, the correlations between residuals were not significant in all three models, indicating no simultaneous change in composition and income. The findings, then, corroborate the segregation hypothesis but do not support the notion of competition.

Patently, the findings demonstrate that the processes operating for Israeli Arabs were considerably different from those operating for noncitizen Arabs. The model for Israeli Arabs lends support to the segregation hypothesis. The model for noncitizen Arabs lends support to the notion of competition as a simultaneous process. Understanding the sources of differences between these two subordinate ethnic groups should provide us with some clues regarding the meaning of segregation and competition in generating labor market discrimination.

Segregation and Competition

Exclusionary closure involves the exercise of power in which one group secures its advantages by closing off opportunities for another group (Murphy 1985; Parkin 1979). Indeed, exclusion entails detrimental outcomes for subordinate groups. The analysis reported in this chapter attempted to expand the understanding of exclusion by examining its potential consequences not only for subordinates but for the superordinate group as well. The analysis was performed within the framework of the competition-segregation model. Proponents of both hypotheses agree that the higher the percentage of subordinates, the lower the income of superordinates in an occupation. They do not agree, however, on the causal dynamics underlying this relationship. According to the segregation thesis, ethnic minorities are denied access to lucrative occupations and are therefore overrepresented in lower-income occupations. According to the competition thesis, the entry of subordinates into an occupation depresses the income of superordinates because members of the former group tend to supply their labor at a lower price (see also Bonacich 1972 and 1976).

Our findings indicate that both mechanisms are empirically significant, albeit for different population groups. Segregation operated in the case of Israeli Arabs in much the way it did for blacks in the United States (Snyder and Hudis 1976). Competition as a simultaneous process, however, prevailed in the case of noncitizen Arabs in Israel. These different findings require further discussion and explanation. It is especially important from a sociological point of view to understand why different mechanisms applied for the two groups. Such an understanding will enable us to trace the social forces that generate various forms of labor market discrimination not only in Israel but in other societies.

The explanation we offer is rooted in the relative status of the two groups vis-à-vis Israeli society. Israeli Arabs enjoy citizenship rights. They benefit from the protection of unions, workers' organizations, and especially from extensive labor relations legislation pertaining to equal pay, minimum wage, and other work-related benefits. Israeli Arabs have been part of the system longer than noncitizen Arabs. They have better knowledge of the labor market and consequently better access to rewards associated with work and occupations. Once Israeli Arabs secure a particular job, they are in a position to demand and to receive pay equal to that of Jewish workers.

Noncitizen Arabs, by contrast, can be viewed as migrant laborers with a tenuous legal position. In fact, their status in the Israeli economy is temporary, and they must periodically renew their work permits. Moreover, they do not belong to trade unions in a society where the overwhelming majority of workers are organized, and they have virtually no usurpatory power (cf. Parkin 1979). Consequently, noncitizen Arabs are hard-pressed to supply their labor at a lower cost than others and to "play the role" of scab labor.

Noncitizen Arabs, relative to other ethnic groups, are far more concentrated at the bottom of the occupational ladder, mainly in the secondary, peripheral segments of the labor market. The consequences of their peculiar occupational distribution, coupled with their unique legal status, are twofold. On one hand, they do not pose a threat to most members of the superordinate ethnic group, especially those in lucrative occupations. On the other hand, they operate in labor markets in which rules of minimum wage, pay, and fringe benefits are least formalized and easily violated. Indeed, opportunities for wage discrimination in this segment of the economy are abundant. These low-status occupations, then, provide fertile grounds for the emergence of competition. Employers are highly interested in recruiting low-price workers, regardless of ascriptive status. The availability of an exploitable ethnic minority such as noncitizen Arabs not only segregates them to lower-status occupations but causes a decline in the income of other workers employed in these occupations.

These conditions of competition have been viewed in sociological literature as central to the emergence of ethnic antagonism. Indeed, Bonacich (1972, 549) has argued that "ethnic antagonism first germinates in a labor market split along ethnic lines. To be split, a labor market must contain at least two groups of workers whose price of labor differs for the same work, or would differ if they did the same work." In a similar vein, Labovitz and Hagedorn (1975) proposed that direct competition between members of a subordinate group and members of superordinate groups is particularly conducive to antagonistic relations. Hence a series of questions arises as to the impact of the conditions illustrated by our findings on general features of Jewish-Arab relations in Israel. More specifically, at issue is whether economic relations have added a new dimension to the unresolved conflict. Although these questions are beyond the scope of this endeavor, their implications will be discussed in the concluding section of the book.

In sum, the findings we observed have general implications regarding the meaning of segregation and competition. Competition is dependent on the existence of some degree of segregation in the labor market. In fact, segregation is a necessary but by no means sufficient condition for the emergence of income discrimination along the principles outlined by the competition hypothesis. The more prestigious and lucrative occupations are monopolized by superordinates, who deny others access to these occupations because of the rewards associated with them. The weaker the position of an ethnic group in the social system, the more likely it is to be shunted away from the more lucrative occupations and pressured to supply its labor at a lower price.

Competition, however, emerges under specific conditions when a group is faced with limited employment opportunities coupled with restricted legal and political recourse, as is often the case with migrant labor. Indeed, this condition distinguishes noncitizen Arabs in Israel from local Israeli Arabs and hence the differential effect each group exerts on income.

5

Income Differentials

The socioeconomic disadvantages faced by racial and ethnic groups have long been of central interest to researchers of social stratification. Consequently, considerable attention has been devoted to trying to understand sources and causes of economic discrimination. Many studies have decomposed the socioeconomic differentials between ethnic and racial groups in an effort to find out whether the economic disadvantages of a subordinate group are a function of its lack of resources, its inferior position in the social structure, discrimination, or a combination of all three (e.g., Almquist 1975; Duncan 1968; Iams and Thornton 1975; Niemi 1974; Reimers 1984; Siegel 1965; Stolzenberg 1975).

Status attainment and human capital models operate on the premise that in modern society educational resources are the major distributor of individuals to occupational positions. Occupational status, in turn, is the most significant determinant of income (e.g., Blau and Duncan 1967; Hauser and Featherman 1977). Ethnic minorities are usually characterized by their limited education, low-status occupations, and low income. Hence the question of whether the low income of subordinate ethnic minorities is a consequence of their limited education and low occupational status or of economic discrimination, and, if both, to what extent each is responsible, has become a central theme in the literature.

The conclusion generally reached is twofold. First, subordinate groups are likely to be segregated in lower-status occupations. They are denied access to lucrative and prestigious occupations (Taeuber et al. 1966; Niemi 1974; Lieberson and Fuguitt 1967; Lieberson 1980; Stolzenberg 1975; Semyonov et al. 1984). Second, members of subordinate ethnic groups are likely to be paid less than superordinate group members even when their occupational status, education, and other "human capital" variables are taken into consideration (Siegel 1965; Thurow 1975; Duncan 1968; Reimers 1984).

Patently, discrimination, whether through occupational segregation or otherwise, has detrimental consequences for the income of subordinate ethnic groups. The findings reported in the previous chapters underscore two major points. First, noncitizen Arabs have been relegated in increasing numbers to lower-status, poorly paid occupations. Second, the massive influx of noncitizen Arabs to lower-status occupations has resulted in the deterioration of the income level of other incumbents in these occupations. The analysis thus far, however, has not dealt with the question of whether and to what extent the income of noncitizen Arabs has been determined by their human capital or by their occupational segregation. Nor has it estimated the socioeconomic costs of their ethnic subordination.

In the analysis that follows, the socioeconomic status of noncitizen Arabs employed in Israel will be compared, first, to Israeli citizens, and second, to Arabs who work in the militarily administered territories of the West Bank and Gaza Strip. From an empirical point of view, such a comparison permits a decomposition of the socioeconomic differentials of noncitizen Arab workers and Israeli citizens, thereby contributing to knowledge of economic discrimination in general and discrimination in Israel in particular. From a theoretical vantage point, the analysis underscores the costs and benefits involved in labor migration. Indeed, by comparing the status of noncitizen Arabs with that of both Israeli citizens and Arabs who work in the militarily administered territories, it becomes possible to specify the trade-offs workers make between occupational status and income. Such analysis casts light on the forces that generate labor migration across communities not only in Israel but in other societies.

Formal and Informal Mechanisms Determining Wages of Noncitizen Arabs

A central consideration in the decision to employ noncitizen Arabs is of course the cost of labor. To protect noncitizens from extreme exploitation, and the local labor force from unwarranted competition, the government of Israel requires that noncitizen Arab workers be paid at least the minimum wage stipulated for all industrial workers in Israel. This requirement is enforced by the Government Employment Service, which is invested with the responsibility to administer the salaries of noncitizen Arabs legally registered for employment in Israel.

To keep track of all wages and social benefit payments in a very fluid labor market, employers must transfer payrolls of their noncitizen Arab employees and once a month appropriate funds to the Payments Division of the Government Employment Service. This agency then deducts taxes and other dues and hands over the remaining sums to the workers (Amir 1985). As a result, the payment of wages to all noncitizen Arabs legally registered for employment in Israel is centralized and records are kept of wages earned and social benefits accrued even when workers change their place of employment.

The procedure established to monitor payments actually does little to ensure Arab workers parity with local workers. Payrolls submitted by employers are rarely examined. "Except for construction workers, it [the Government Employment Service] simply does not check employers' calculations, except to ensure that the general minimum wage is honoured for the standard workday" (Shalev 1986). The emphasis on daily wages ignores many salary components, such as industry- or company-specific increments, bonuses, and overtime payments, that account for a substantial portion of the income of unskilled and skilled workers. The absence of these payments from the salaries of noncitizen Arabs may contribute to the large income disparity with Israeli workers.

Concrete evidence of a wage differential and its sources was provided by a recent survey of twelve public and private firms that employ noncitizen Arabs (Laor 1986). The survey revealed that in most cases starting wages of noncitizen Arabs were equal to the wages earned by Israeli workers in similar jobs. Substantial differences existed, however, in the level of wage supplements. Noncitizen Arabs were less likely than local workers to receive productivity bonuses, family allowances, and seniority increments. In many cases noncitizen Arabs were required to work more hours for the same daily wages. Noncitizen Arabs were also unlikely to advance into more rewarding jobs. In only two of the firms surveyed was their advancement determined in the same manner as that of Israeli workers. In other firms advancement was either slow or totally nonexistent.

A substantial wage differential is created as a result of the differential treatment of noncitizen Arabs and Israeli workers who occupy similar jobs. A comparison of gross and net wages in a number of industrial firms and service organizations revealed that in some cases the wages of Israeli workers were 30 percent higher than the wages of noncitizen Arabs in the same jobs. In the companies surveyed the gross earnings of Israeli workers were 17 percent higher on the average, and, because higher taxes are levied on noncitizen Arabs, the net earnings were 25 percent higher. These figures are based on information provided by companies willing to participate in the survey and thus should be taken as conservative estimates. It is quite likely that the terms of employment for noncitizen Arabs in other firms are even less rewarding. Furthermore, the firms surveyed all employed workers legally registered with the Government Employment Service. Consequently, some minimum standards would have been maintained. Many noncitizen Arab workers in Israel are employed illegally (without registering), usually by small employers. In this case there is no official monitoring of their wages and large-scale exploitation may take place.

The income gap between Israeli workers and noncitizen Arab workers is evident in the figures in table 5.1. Furthermore, the income gap is evident within each of the nine broad occupational categories. It is interesting that the income differentials were substantial in 1969 and remained so through 1981, though the gaps had been declining over the years. The gaps are also somewhat more pronounced in the higher-status occupational categories than in the low-status manual ones. Because occupational segregation between Israelis and noncitizen Arabs exists within occupational categories, it is important to compare the income of the two populations in a more systematic and rigorous manner. The analysis that follows thus takes into consideration both a more detailed occupational classification (eighty-three occupational categories) and other population characteristics such as education and age.

TABLE 5.1 Daily Income of Noncitizen Arabs as Percentages of Daily Income of Israelis and Jewish Workers across Occupational Categories, 1969, 1975, and 1981

| | 1969 | | 1975 | | 1981 | |
| | Income of Noncitizen Arabs as Percentage of Income of | | Income of Noncitizen Arabs as Percentage of Income of | | Income of Noncitizen Arabs as Percentage of Income of | |
Occupational Category	Israelis	Jews	Israelis	Jews	Israelis	Jews
Scientific and academic	38.0[a]	38.0[a]	58.4[a]	58.2[a]	80.1[a]	79.9[a]
Professional and technical	—[b]	—	69.1[a]	69.0[a]	66.2[a]	65.6[a]
Administrators and managers	—	—	46.1[a]	46.0[a]	76.6[a]	76.6[a]
Clerical	—	—	77.6[a]	77.4[a]	71.5[a]	71.2[a]
Sales	41.7	40.8	64.6	64.5	60.4	59.5
Service	33.8	33.7	81.2	80.6	82.3	81.9
Skilled and semiskilled	49.7[c]	48.9[c]	88.5	87.9	82.9	81.4
Unskilled	42.6[c]	42.6[c]	93.1	91.0	90.2	87.0
Agricultural	47.2	46.5	86.2	84.4	68.6	68.1

[a]Estimates are based on a very small number of noncitizen Arabs employed in this occupational category.
[b]Data not available.
[c]Category does not completely overlap with the definition of 1975 and 1981.

Comparison of Noncitizen Arabs and Israeli Citizens

This analysis centers, first, on a comparison of the socioeconomic status of noncitizen Arabs and Israeli workers. Characteristics of the subpopulations included in the analysis were estimated from the occupational distributions generated in 1981. Individuals were then grouped into two-digit occupations, and means of the variables employed in the analysis were calculated for each subpopulation within each occupation.

The four variables used to decompose socioeconomic differentials between subpopulations were income (i.e., earnings per day),[1] occupational status (i.e., Tyree's [1981] 100-point socioeconomic scale for occupations in Israel), education (i.e., years of formal schooling), and age (in years). The analysis was restricted to the male labor force aged fourteen and over both in Israel and in the militarily administered territories. The first question is whether noncitizen Arab workers differ in socioeconomic status from Israeli workers. To answer this question the mean values of the variables included in the analysis were compared for the two subpopulations. The values for Israeli citizens are presented in column 1 of table 5.2, and the figures for noncitizen Arab workers are displayed in column 2 of table 5.2.

The figures in table 5.2 clearly reflect the socioeconomic disparities between the two groups. Israelis are advantaged over noncitizen Arabs in every status variable included in the table. They earn almost twice as much as noncitizen Arabs, their average occupational status is higher by 20 points than that of noncitizen Arabs, and their educational level exceeds that of noncitizen Arabs by more than four years. Furthermore, noncitizen Arabs in the labor force are considerably younger than Israeli citizens.

Decomposing Income Differentials

Although the differences between the groups are of interest, it is not clear to what extent the lower income of noncitizen Arabs is a function of their inferior occupational status, education, and age or their ethnic subordination. To arrive at an answer, the socio-

---

1. Daily income for Israeli citizens was estimated by dividing weekly income by seven, thus providing the most conservative estimate.

TABLE 5.2. *Estimated Socioeconomic Differentials between Citizens and Noncitizen Arabs in Israel (standard deviations in parentheses)*

Variables	Israeli Citizens (1)	(Jews)	Noncitizen Arabs in Israel (2)
Daily income (in Israeli shekels)	181.87 (63.80)	(184.91)	108.31 (20.17)
Occupational status	45.58 (19.82)	(45.98)	22.69 (8.33)
Education	11.48 (3.25)	(11.55)	6.49 (1.11)
Age	39.08 (3.44)	(39.12)	30.90 (2.38)
Weighted n	517,120	(498,815)	79,841

economic differentials between the groups were decomposed using Duncan's indirect standardization procedure (1968). This procedure seems particularly appropriate given the logic embodied in the research question. The logic is to ask what the occupational status or income of a subject population (here noncitizen Arabs) would be if their socioeconomic attainment were determined in the same way as that of the standard population (here Israeli citizens). In this hypothetical case the minority is exposed to the same conditions and processes that determine the socioeconomic attainment of the majority.[2] The procedure thus "forces" the mean values of noncitizen Arab workers through the weighted regression equations predicting occupational status and income of the Israeli population.

The decomposition procedure can be expressed by the following statistical notation

$$\overline{Y}_S - \overline{Y}_R = \sum_{i=1}^{n} b_{iS} (\overline{X}_{iS} - \overline{X}_{iR}) + k$$

where S and R stand, respectively, for Israeli citizens and noncitizen Arab workers and the $\overline{Y}$s are the mean values of the dependent

2. It seems implausible to center on any other hypothetical situation or research question. Duncan's procedure seems most appropriate for this specific research, and for this reason alone it was preferred over other methods of decomposition (e.g., Iams and Thornton 1975).

TABLE 5.3 Estimated Mean Occupational Status and Daily Income of Noncitizen Arab Workers in Israel Obtained through Indirect Standardization, with Israeli Citizens as Standard Population

	Occupational Status[a] (1)	Daily Income[b] (2)	Daily Income[c] (3)
Initial gap	22.90	73.56	73.56
Gap remaining after standardization	33.37	62.24	35.25
Actual mean	22.68	108.31	108.31
Estimated mean obtained through standardization	12.21	119.63	146.63
Gap due to ethnicity	10.47	11.32	38.32

[a]Estimates were obtained through a regression equation in which occupational status was a function of education and age.

[b]Estimates were obtained through a regression equation in which income was a function of occupation and age.

[c]Estimates were obtained through a regression equation in which income was a function of occupation, age, and education.

variables (in this specific investigation occupational status and income). The $\overline{X}$s are the mean values of the antecedent variables, weighted by the regression coefficients obtained from the regression equation for the standard population (here Israelis). The second term on the right side of the equation—k—is the component due to ethnicity and is interpreted as the discrimination component. The results obtained by this decomposition procedure are presented in table 5.3.

Column 1 of table 5.3 pertains to the occupational disparities between the two groups. The 22.9-point gap in occupational status indicates extreme segregation between Israelis and noncitizen Arabs. In fact, when the two groups are compared across eighty-seven occupational categories using an index of dissimilarity (Taeuber and Taeuber 1965), the index has a value of 66.7. In other words, two-thirds of Israelis or noncitizen Arabs would have to change occupations to arrive at equal occupational distributions. Considering the limited education and comparatively young age of noncitizen Arabs, however, one would expect the observed occupational gap (22.9 points) to be at least 9 points higher. That is, the occupational status of noncitizen Arabs in the Israeli labor market is actually higher than one would expect had attainment been determined by education and age, as it is in the general labor force. Apparently the occupational segregation of noncitizen Arabs is so extreme and their status so low that their educational level is irrelevant for their jobs in Israel. Indeed, noncitizen Arabs are not competing with Israelis for the low-status, undesirable jobs available to them. It is also possible that selectivity in the acquisition of education produces a stronger positive correlation between education and ability among Israelis than among Arabs and that Israelis with an educational level as low as that of the average noncitizen Arab thus hold very low status jobs.

The results obtained when the income gap between Israelis and noncitizen Arabs are decomposed are presented in columns 2 and 3 of table 5.3. The income disparity between the two groups is considerable. It reached 73.6 Israeli shekels (higher by more than two-thirds than the average income of noncitizen Arabs). The decomposition procedure reveals that most of the income differential between the two groups is attributable to occupational segregation. When the low occupational status and young age of noncitizen Arab workers are considered, however, some portion of the income gap is attributable to ethnicity. Had the earnings of noncitizen Arabs been determined as they are for Israeli citizens, the income of Arabs would have been somewhat higher.

Comparing "Movers" with "Stayers"

At this point it seems meaningful to compare the socioeconomic status of noncitizen Arabs employed in Israel (movers) with those employed in the administered territories of the West Bank and Gaza Strip (stayers). Such an analysis underscores the potential economic benefits noncitizen Arabs gain upon joining the Israeli economy. Indeed, noncitizen Arabs, like migrant laborers, search for jobs in Israel because they lack economic opportunities in the administered territories.

Reports by the Bank of Israel Research Department (Zakai 1985) illustrate rather clearly the economic benefits noncitizen Arabs may gain upon joining the Israeli economy. Overall, as well as within economic sectors, the wages of noncitizen Arabs employed in Israel are considerably higher than those of Arabs who are employed in the administered territories (see table 5.4). The differences between these two groups of workers, however, have been declining over the years. This decline is perhaps an indicator that

TABLE 5.4 Ratio of Wages of Noncitizen Arabs Employed in Israel to Those of Arabs Employed in Judea-Samaria and Gaza, by Industry and by Year

	1970	1972	1975	1977	1978	1979	1980	1981	1982
Judea-Samaria									
Total	173.5	147.8	126.1	110.9	112.0	119.4	116.6	115.5	114.8
Agriculture	195.6	141.6	115.2	97.7	95.5	97.6	102.1	109.3	117.0
Industry	187.9	130.3	152.3	135.5	139.2	135.4	132.4	126.4	124.9
Construction	197.0	128.4	115.0	102.6	101.7	106.4	105.4	109.1	107.5
Other	134.6	124.6	110.6	102.0	106.9	113.5	106.8	105.8	102.3
Gaza District									
Total	201.7	170.9	118.3	113.3	114.7	138.4	122.1	103.5	105.1
Agriculture	214.0	158.4	123.1	116.3	125.7	126.3	123.9	120.4	120.6
Industry	282.9	175.0	142.8	141.2	148.6	146.1	148.9	160.0	162.7
Construction	312.5	203.1	119.7	116.8	113.2	124.2	109.8	118.2	123.5
Other	167.6	175.7	101.5	105.3	104.9	137.8	110.4	86.8	88.4

Source: Bank of Israel (1985).

the two economies—those of Israel and of the West Bank and Gaza Strip—are becoming more and more integrated and interdependent.

Based on the findings reported in table 5.4 and especially the income superiority of noncitizen Arabs employed in Israel, it seems plausible to ask what the attainment of noncitizen Arabs would be if their occupational status and income were determined in the same way as that of Arabs who are employed in the administered territories. Stated differently, what would be the expected attainment of noncitizen Arabs in the Israeli economy had they been employed in the administered territories rather than in Israel?[3]

The answer to this question is suggested in table 5.5, in which the socioeconomic status of the two groups—movers and stayers—is compared. A comparison of the mean values of noncitizen Arabs who were employed in Israel and those of Arabs who remained to work in the administered territories indicates that the former en-

3. It is also possible to ask hypothetically what the attainment of Arabs currently employed in the administered territories would be had they been rewarded as noncitizen Arabs are who are employed in Israel. From a theoretical point of view, this is not an interesting question. A statistical calculation of this issue, however, resulted in similar findings (and conclusions) to those reported in table 5.6.

TABLE 5.5 Estimated Socioeconomic Differentials between Noncitizen Arabs and Arabs in the Administered Territories (standard deviations in parentheses)

	Noncitizen Arabs in Israel	Arabs in the Administered Territories
	(1)	(2)
Daily income (in Israeli shekels)	108.31	100.38
	(20.17)	(46.16)
Occupational status	22.69	35.48
	(8.33)	(19.15)
Education (in years)	6.49	7.69
	(1.11)	(3.30)
Age	30.90	33.33
	(2.38)	(5.96)
Weighted *n*	70,841	90,072

joyed somewhat higher income, even though the latter were older, better educated, and held higher-status occupations (their rankings differed by more than 12 points). Thus it appears that although noncitizen Arabs sacrifice occupational status, they compensate for this loss by increasing their income upon joining the Israeli economy.

The issue needs further, more careful analysis. The extent to which noncitizen Arabs may have gained or lost socioeconomic status must be established. Duncan's decomposition procedure (1968), discussed in detail earlier, provides a way of estimating the extent to which the socioeconomic status of average noncitizen Arabs who "migrated" to Israel increased or decreased compared to that of Arabs employed in the administered territories. In this procedure, the mean values of the characteristics of noncitizen Arabs were "forced" through the weighted regression equations predicting occupational status and income of workers in the administered territories. The results of this analysis are presented in table 5.6.

The findings provide firm support for the argument that labor migration may be costly in one dimension but beneficial in another. Migration to Israel extracts some costs to noncitizen Arabs in occupational status. Had these workers found jobs in the administered territories, their occupational status would have increased by almost 5 points (40 percent of the initial gap in

TABLE 5.6 Estimated Mean Occupational Status and Daily Income of Noncitizen Arab Workers in Israel Obtained through Indirect Standardization, with Arabs in the Administered Territories as Standard Population

	Occupational Status[a] (1)	Daily Income[b] (2)	Daily Income[c] (3)
Initial gap	12.8	7.93	7.93
Gap remaining after standardization	7.69	15.75	9.57
Actual mean	22.68	108.31	108.31
Estimated mean obtained through standardization	27.79	84.63	90.81
Gap due to "migration"	5.11	23.68	17.50

[a]Estimates were obtained through a regression equation in which occupational status was a function of education and age.

[b]Estimates were obtained through a regression equation in which income was a function of occupation and age.

[c]Estimates were obtained through a regression equation in which income was a function of occupation, age, and education.

occupational status between the two groups). Noncitizen Arabs are "overpaid," however, in comparison to Arabs who work in the administered territories. Given the occupational status, education, and age of noncitizen Arab workers, their income is higher by 45.5 percent than it would be in the administered territories.

Noncitizen Arabs, like migrant laborers elsewhere, have to compromise to hold the least desirable, low-status occupations in the "host" country. They are, without question, segregated in occupations at the bottom of the occupational ladder. In contrast, Arabs in the administered territories have to produce incumbents for positions across the entire occupational spectrum. That is, they have to produce physicians, engineers, university professors, teachers, and clerks, as well as garbage collectors and skilled and unskilled manual workers. As a result, both the mean occupational status and the standard deviation for Arabs in the administered territories are considerably higher than those for noncitizen Arabs employed in Israel. Also, the index of dissimilarity between noncitizen Arabs and Arabs employed in the administered territories reaches a value of 57.

It is important to emphasize that a selectivity bias probably occurs in that the movers and stayers are not random samples of the same populations.[4] Apparently, better educated, older workers in the administered territories have greater access to jobs at various rungs in the occupational ladder. Arabs employed in Israel are relegated to lower-status occupations relinquished by Israeli citizens. Their income, however, is higher by far than it could possibly be in the West Bank and Gaza Strip. In sum, noncitizen Arabs are disadvantaged economically in comparison to Israelis but are advantaged compared to Arabs living and working in the administered territories.

Explaining Income Differentials

The analysis in this chapter clearly demonstrates that noncitizen Arabs, like other subordinate ethnic groups, are segregated at the bottom of the occupational ladder. Nevertheless, when their educational level and age are taken into consideration, their occupational status is somewhat higher than one would expect were their attainment determined as it is for others in the Israeli labor force. Patently, the low educational level of noncitizen Arabs is irrelevant in the occupations available to them in Israel. The extreme occupational segregation of noncitizen Arabs does not fully account, however, for their lower income. Some portion of the income gap between them and Israeli citizens is attributable to ethnicity. The ethnic origins of noncitizen Arabs coupled with their unique legal and political status evidently have had detrimental consequences for their socioeconomic status in Israel.

Lack of opportunities and legal restrictions have indeed contributed to producing income discrimination against noncitizen Arabs. But other conditions have also contributed. Considering the low cost of living in the West Bank and Gaza Strip, it is understandable that noncitizen Arab workers would be "willing" to settle for lower wages. Furthermore, many noncitizen Arabs are from rural areas and may consider their income in Israel to be a supplement to their earnings from farming (or vice versa). All these factors play a major role in producing the conditions that generate income discrimination of a subordinate population vis-à-vis the "host" economy.

4. We do not believe that the bias is large enough to affect the results.

Decomposition of the socioeconomic differentials between noncitizen Arabs and workers in the administered territories helps to explain why Arabs turn to jobs in Israel. Lack of economic opportunities in the militarily administered territories motivated them to take their low-status positions. Migration appears to cost noncitizen Arabs in occupational status but to provide them with greater income. Apparently, labor migration across economies should be understood as exchange processes in which migrant laborers have to trade off occupational status for income.

6

A Comparative Perspective on Noncitizen Arabs

The findings reported thus far indicate rather clearly that social and market conditions are major determinants of the status of noncitizen Arabs in the Israeli economy. These conditions influence not only the permeation of noncitizen Arabs into the labor market but also the ways in which their employment affects the social organization of the Israeli labor force. Despite the unique social and political position of noncitizen Arabs in Israel, both their integration and their impact can be understood within a general theoretical framework and, more specifically, in the context of theoretical formulations centered on ethnic stratification of the labor market. In accordance with this perspective, it appears that noncitizen Arabs employed in Israel are subject to forces similar to those exerted on subordinate ethnic minorities and foreign workers in other industrial countries. In the analysis that follows the occupational and industrial distribution of noncitizen Arabs and foreign workers in other countries is compared to demonstrate the general applicability of this thesis.

As noted at the outset of this book, the term *migrant labor* is used to describe nonnationals in a host of work situations. Recent volumes on migrant labor (e.g., Böhning 1984; Rogers 1985; Lewis 1985) have enumerated a considerable number of categories of migrants. Accordingly, one may distinguish between regular (legal) and irregular (illegal) migrants. Within the category of regulars, differentiation is based on whether work is restricted, stay is limited, or residence is permitted. There are some migrants whose stay and employment are essentially unrestricted. Such is the case for migrants within the Common Nordic Labour Market and for citizens of countries that are members of the European Economic Community. Similar arrangements exist in other regions as well (e.g., certain West African states; the Syrian Arab Republic and Iraq, which have a similar policy vis-à-vis citizens of other Arab states). Certain migrants in the United States and in Western Europe have such rights after living in their respective countries for an extended period of time.

A second large category of migrants, referred to as contract migrants, are distinguished by the limitations on their stay and employment. A variety of arrangements are possible, including year-round permits, such as those held by many nonnationals in Western Europe and those held by temporary and seasonal workers whose stay is limited to a relatively short time and who are permitted to work in specific jobs. The latter arrangement is characteristic of many nonnationals in agriculture in France, Mexicans in the southwestern United States, and many nonnational Africans employed in the mines in South Africa. An additional category of workers is distinguished by their residence and includes frontier or commuter workers. Unlike most migrant labor, these workers live in their own countries but cross the border regularly for employment purposes. By definition, such an arrangement requires geographic proximity and therefore arises under specific circumstances. Typical of such labor are the Italian sojourners in Switzerland and blacks who commute to South Africa. This category also comes closest to describing the legal arrangements under which noncitizen Arabs are employed in Israel. The unique characteristic of this situation, of course, is that the nonnational workers do not live within the borders of the host society and as a result have contact with the local population and institutions which is limited, for the most part, to the labor market.

These distinctions not withstanding, we will use the term *migrant* in the remainder of our discussion in a generic and much simplified sense. It will refer to nonnationals who are present in a particular labor market irrespective of their motivations or those of policy makers in the host society regarding the purpose or duration of their stay. We take this approach because the issue of migrant labor is of secondary importance in the present context and therefore does not warrant a drawn-out treatment. More important, we believe that the lack of political and, often, legal rights characteristic of most migrant workers is an important determinant in their position in the labor market. Finally, it is assumed here that migrant labor, irrespective of the specific legal arrangement, is driven by labor market demand and hence that fairly similar processes are likely to evolve in the realm of employment.

Indeed, the phenomenon of migrant or guest labor cannot be comprehended fully without considering structural changes that have occurred in both the economy and the labor force of advanced industrial societies. Since the middle of the century, industrial countries have experienced economic growth and have, by and large, exhausted their local labor reserve (Böhning 1972; Power 1979). These countries are further characterized by expanding opportunities in higher-status—white-collar and professional—occupations. Rising educational levels have further fostered expectations for intrinsically more rewarding and prestigious jobs (Pollard 1979). In addition, most industrial societies have reached some form of consensus with respect to employment security, wages, and welfare rights of citizen wage earners (Castells 1978; Rex 1979). Consequently, the local labor force has become less responsive to changes in the demand for workers and is unwilling to fill many onerous, low-paying jobs. These constraints generate the need for cheap labor to fill mostly seasonal, temporary, and insecure jobs (Gorz 1970; Piore 1979; Lewis 1985). Hence the demand for migrant labor can arise from a physical shortage of labor, as was the case in Western Europe in the 1950s and 1960s, or from a relative shortage in which not enough inactive persons can be attracted under the prevailing conditions (wage rates, types of jobs, and the like). The latter is probably descriptive of the situation in the United States and in present-day Europe, limited though labor migration may be.

The features of the labor market just described generally lead to the view that the entry of migrant workers into the occupational system is a result of specific and unique labor shortages in particular economic sectors and is thus a temporary solution. Such a view suggests high sectoral and occupational concentration during the initial stages of contact. As time passes, however, migrant labor comes to be viewed as an integral and possibly indispensable part of the labor market. As more employers realize the potential benefits from employing migrant labor, and as greater numbers of native workers shift into expanding and more lucrative sections of the economy, it is expected that migrant labor will flow into additional economic sectors and become less industrially concentrated. The entry of migrant labor, then, sets off a dynamic process whereby migrant workers penetrate large parts of the industrial structure. Hence it is expected that the industrial distribution of migrant labor and the local labor force will grow more similar and occupational differences will remain fairly stable.

Migrant labor is expected to be occupationally concentrated and to be located at the bottom of the occupational hierarchy. This perception arises as a result of the personal characteristics of the migrants. Coming from less developed societies, the migrants are less educated and less skilled than the host population. In addition, they are limited by language and cultural barriers. Indeed, according to Piore (1979), migrant workers are employed in the secondary labor market and are a target of economic exploitation because of these characteristics. If personal characteristics were the sole barriers to occupational success, however, one would expect that as time passed and migrants learned the language and improved their skills they would advance in the occupational structure. This does not generally occur in the case of guest labor. Additional forces are involved, first and foremost the legal and political status of nonresident workers. Castells has noted that "the basic contradiction concerning immigrants, is one which opposes them not directly to capital, but to the State apparatus of capital and to the political status given to them in its institutions" (1978, 33). Lack of citizenship rights puts migrant labor in a position in which negotiation regarding the conditions of work is even more difficult than it is for other subordinate groups. Alien workers are frequently required to obtain state-issued work permits, labor legislation may not apply equally to nonresidents, and they are usually unorganized and therefore less successful in securing even those rights and benefits to which they are legally entitled. Other factors such as direct discrimination by employers or refusal of endogenous workers to be supervised by aliens further contribute to the job subordination of noncitizen employees (Castles and Kosack 1973).[1]

1. The process differs, of course, in the case of the so-called brain drain. Nonnational professional and technical workers are often admitted for employment in their occupations or in any case find employment in the higher rungs of the occupational ladder.

The above-mentioned features create the predicament of migrant workers. Though their industrial distribution is likely to become more diverse over time, their position in the occupational structure is unlikely to improve much. Although the skills of migrant labor are upgraded with the passage of time, and some individuals shift to more rewarding occupations, their advances on the occupational ladder are unlikely to outdistance those of local workers, and the occupational gap between the groups remains. To study these processes it is necessary to compare changes in the industrial and occupational placement of nonnational workers with parallel processes in the local population.

Occupational Distribution

Perhaps the most salient finding to emerge from a comparison of occupational distributions of foreign (guest) workers across countries is that they are significantly similar. In table 6.1 occupations are classified into four categories: nonmanual, skilled, semiskilled, and unskilled. This broad classification enables a cross-national comparison. Figures for European countries represent the period of expanding migration prior to the rather sudden change in policy that took place in 1973–74. As is evident from the figures, foreign workers in all five countries were overwhelmingly concentrated in manual jobs and underrepresented in nonmanual occupations compared with the local labor force. The extreme differences between local and noncitizen workers are clearly revealed by the index of dissimilarity presented in the last row of the table. A large proportion of noncitizen workers tended to fill unskilled occupations, and more than two-thirds held either unskilled or semiskilled jobs. Indeed, noncitizen Arabs and foreign workers in Europe and the United States appear to be relegated to the least desirable, low-status occupations.

As we have noted at various points in our discussion, we believe the position of noncitizen Arabs in the occupational structure is considerably affected by their tenuous legal and political status. Nonresident status is inherently temporary. Even workers employed in Israel for fifteen years are not given tenure and can be

---

This group, however, constitutes only a small proportion of migrant labor (about 7.5 percent in the United States in 1979) (see Böhning 1984, 50).

TABLE 6.1 *Percentage Distribution of Noncitizen and Local Workers in Five Countries across Major Occupational Categories*

	Israel (1982)		Switzerland (1960)	
	Noncitizen Arabs	Local Employees	Foreign Employees	Local Employees
Nonmanual	3.8	52.9	15.0	52.0
Skilled manual	9.0	15.5	25.0	18.5
Semiskilled manual	29.6	15.7	37.0	22.5
Unskilled manual	57.6	15.9	23.0	7.0
Total percent	100.0	100.0	100.0	100.0
Index of dissimilarity	55.6		37.0	

Source: Switzerland, France, and Germany, Castles and Kosack (1973), tables III.4, III.15, and III.16. United States, Brown and Shue (1983), tables 8.1 and 8.2.
ªCalculated for two categories.

fired with short notice. To a certain extent this is the result of their lack of contact with labor unions. In the early 1970s the Federation of Jewish Workers in Israel attempted to persuade noncitizen Arabs to join the unions both to protect themselves from exploitation by employers and to protect local workers from competition. Noncitizen Arabs were reluctant to join for political reasons and possibly because they were not familiar with the benefits of worker organizations. Currently, they are legally permitted to organize but tend not to. Although noncitizen Arabs are represented on worker committees in some establishments, in most cases they are not and do not receive the union protection enjoyed by other workers. Their grievances are often submitted to and handled by the state-run employment offices. Furthermore, as noted earlier, official work permits are required of noncitizen workers employed in Israel. This requirement affords the state a large degree of control over where the person will be employed and the extent of mobility among jobs.

This situation is not unique to Israel, of course. Indeed, all Western European countries that import labor have policies and regulations that control the entry, movement, and activities of guest (or migrant) labor. During the 1960s the status of guest workers in the Federal Republic of Germany, especially those from nations that were not members of the European Economic Community, was precarious. They were required to hold work permits, were often limited to a particular factory and job, and were some-

France (1967)		Germany (1968)		United States (1975)	
Foreign Employees	*Local Employees*	*Foreign Employees*	*Local Employees*	*Apprehended Illegal Aliens*	*Local Employees*
6.3	36.6	8.2	43.7	5.4	49.9
25.2		20.4		15.3	13.1
36.6	63.4	36.7	56.3	25.1	15.2
31.9		34.7		54.2	21.8
100.0	100.0	100.0	100.0	100.0	100.0
	30.3[a]		35.5[a]		44.5

times restricted to certain geographical areas (Reimann and Reimann 1979). Those who were employed were granted equality in labor legislation and welfare laws. In Switzerland, temporary residents and seasonal workers are still required to hold work permits. They are renewed if the situation in the labor market allows, but special permits are needed to change occupations or jobs (Hoffman-Nowotny et al. 1979). The Netherlands passed a law on foreign workers in 1976 which limited to twenty the number of new migrant workers that could work for any one employer. This law applied primarily to Mediterranean workers and in effect restricted their social and geographic movement. As Bovenkerk (1979, 131) noted, "Thus, Mediterraneans in the Netherlands can be unambiguously characterized as a fixed subproletariat."

As a result of their low status, nonnational laborers are considerably more vulnerable and have more limited options in the labor market than local residents. Indeed, this inequality is built into the system and is an integral part of the market process. In Israel, as in other countries, it is openly declared that noncitizen Arabs are to be employed only when Israeli employees cannot be found. In other words, the former are generally recruited into jobs vacated by the latter.

In referring to the migration of Mexican workers to the United States, Portes (1981) noted that the majority of workers are employed in the secondary labor market, where they are recruited mostly because of the low wages they accept. Their judicial status is tenuous, and they are hired primarily by ethnicity not skill. They enter mostly short-term or dead-end jobs and are not part of a promotional ladder. Castles (1984, 138) described a similar situation regarding migrants in West Germany: "On the whole, foreign workers in West Germany do not have very much chance of getting out of their original circumstances as industrial manual workers or doing the least desirable service jobs." Similar outcomes reported for Britain and France seem to echo the processes outlined earlier regarding the concentration of noncitizen Arabs in low-skill manual jobs. Hence, although the magnitude of disadvantage appears to be greater for noncitizen Arabs employed in Israel than for foreign groups in other countries, the patterns of ethnic occupational differentiation in Israel and in other industrial countries share substantial similarities.

Industrial Distribution

Table 6.2 presents the industrial distribution of host labor and foreign labor (noncitizen Arabs) in Israel. The entry of noncitizen Arab workers into the Israeli labor market was characterized by industrial concentration. Approximately 80 percent of the noncitizen Arabs who worked in Israel in 1969 were employed in either construction or agriculture. Indeed, throughout the period, half of all noncitizen Arabs were employed in the construction industry. Between 1969 and 1982 the figures were only slightly reduced, from 54.4 percent to 51 percent. Construction work is physically demanding, seasonal, and carried out by many contractors and subcontractors. It was therefore particularly suited to noncitizen workers, many of whom did not obtain employment certificates and were recruited directly by contractors or acquaintances.

Stability in the construction industry has been substantial, despite change in the distribution of noncitizen Arabs among other industries. There was a steady decline in agriculture, down from 24.3 percent in 1969 to 12.0 percent in 1982. Concomitantly, the proportion of noncitizen Arabs employed in manufacturing rose to 19 percent in 1982, and their representation in service industries expanded as well. Taken as a whole, these processes resulted in less industrial concentration of the group. One way of measuring the concentration, or, conversely, the division of labor,

TABLE 6.2 Percentage Distribution of the Endogenous (Jewish and Arab) and Noncitizen Arab Labor Force by Industry Sector in 1969, 1975, and 1982

Industrial Sector	1969		1975		1982	
	Endogenous Population	Noncitizen Arab	Endogenous Population	Noncitizen Arab	Endogenous Population	Noncitizen Arab
Agriculture	10.5	24.3	6.4	14.0	5.9	12.0
Manufacturing	27.3	11.6	25.7	18.6	24.5	19.2
Construction	8.3	54.4	8.3	54.5	6.4	51.0
Transportation and communications	7.7	2.0	7.2	1.7	6.7	2.0
Trade and finance	18.5	2.1	19.0	5.1	20.9	5.6
Personal and public services	27.7	5.6	33.4	6.1	35.6	10.2
Total	100.0	100.0	100.0	100.0	100.0	100.0
N	990,190	9,380	1,116,006	66,041	1,286,932	75,818
Index of concentration[a]	0.05	0.24	0.08	0.23	0.08	0.19
Index of dissimilarity[a]	59.9		53.8		50.7	

[a]See text for explanation of the measures.

would be to compare the actual distribution to a hypothetical distribution such as equiprobability. The measure differentiates between two polar situations. At one extreme the whole labor force is concentrated in one industrial category, in which case the measure takes on a value of one. At the other extreme the labor force is equally divided among all categories. Such lack of concentration is assigned a value of zero.[2] Comparing the findings for the endogenous and noncitizen Arab population, we find the latter group to be substantially more concentrated. The trend over the years, however, has been toward greater diversification. The value of concentration for noncitizen Arabs was five times greater than for Israelis in 1969, but only two and a half times greater in 1982.

An alternative and more inherently meaningful procedure is to compare the distribution of noncitizen Arab workers by industry to that of the local population. This is carried out here using the index of dissimilarity (D). The index was calculated at three different points in time, and figures are presented in the last row of table 6.2. Apparently, sectoral dissimilarity decreased over the thirteen-year period. The value of 59.9 in 1969 should be interpreted to mean that 60 percent of the labor force in either group would have to be shifted to attain equal industrial distribution. Changes that took place during the period from 1969 to 1982, especially the penetration of noncitizen Arabs into manufacturing and services, reduced the overall differences in industrial distribution between the two groups.

The largest changes took place between 1969 and 1975, a period of rapid expansion in the number of noncitizen Arabs participating in the Israeli economy. Although large numbers still went into agriculture, a higher proportion turned to manufacturing. There was also a substantial increase in the proportion employed in the trade and finance sector. Here they hold mostly cleaning and

---

2. The measure of concentration or division of labor is $1 - \{\Sigma X^2 / (\Sigma X)^2\}$ where X is the number of persons in each category of the labor market classification. The measure was proposed by Gibbs and Martin (1962) and more recently was used by Simpson et al. (1982). Maximum diversity, or the upper limit of the measure, is dependent on the number of categories in the classification and is generally calculated as $1 - 1/k$, where k is the number of categories. For our measure to range from zero to one, with higher values representing greater concentration, the final measure was calculated as (maximum diversity − observed diversity)/maximum diversity.

maintenance jobs in service establishments. Between 1975 and 1982 the category with the greatest proportional growth of noncitizen Arabs was personal and public services. Once again, these are mostly maintenance, sanitation, and gardening jobs in local governments and the hotel and restaurant business. By 1982, then, only 12 percent were in agriculture, 19 percent were in manufacturing, and some 18 percent were in the tertiary sector. Nevertheless, dissimilarity remained very high (50.7), indicating that even after thirteen years of contact noncitizen Arabs were not actually integrated into the economic structure and their employment in construction still remained a major feature of their participation in the Israeli economy.

Table 6.3 presents the industrial distribution of host and guest labor in three European countries. Figures portraying the industrial distribution of the labor force in European countries show overrepresentation of migrant labor in particular industrial sectors in each of the three countries. In West Germany there has been a large concentration in manufacturing and construction. Eighty-six percent of all migrant laborers were in these two sectors in 1969. These figures were reduced, however, during the 1970s, with most of the decline taking place in construction. Migrant labor in France was overrepresented in manufacturing and construction, as it was in Switzerland. Nevertheless, in both countries a sizable proportion of the migrant labor was employed in service industries. More generally, migrant labor was more industrially concentrated in Germany than in the other two countries but was considerably more concentrated in all countries than the local population. Shifts in industrial composition similar to those experienced in Israel took place only in Germany, where the concentration of migrant labor declined from 0.36 in 1969 to 0.27 in 1981. Concomitantly, the differences between the local population and the aliens was reduced, as indicated by the values of the index of dissimilarity. In France, where a shorter period was examined, no noticeable changes took place. By 1968, migrant labor was fairly dispersed among the industrial sectors, and the situation did not change much during the early 1970s. In Switzerland the index of dissimilarity declined slightly from 27.8 in 1972 to 25.5 in 1981, indicating a tendency toward greater industrial integration. Here too, however, migrant labor was rela-

TABLE 6.3 *Percentage Distribution of the Host and Migrant Labor Force, by Industry, in Germany, France, and Switzerland (various years)*

Industrial Sector	Germany[a]				France				Switzerland			
	1969		1981		1968		1975		1972		1981	
	Host	Migrant	Host	Migrant	Host	Migrant	Host	Migrant	Host	Migrant	Host	Migrant
Agriculture, forestry, fishing	1.6	1.3	1.1	1.0	15.1	8.7	10.3	5.7	9.0	2.6	8.9	2.1
Manufacturing, mining, energy	45.4	64.3	41.3	59.0	29.4	36.0	28.8	37.7	35.2	39.2	32.0	41.9
Construction	8.2	21.7	7.8	10.5	9.0	30.0	7.7	25.8	3.4	27.2	2.4	18.5
Transport, communications	5.8	2.6	4.9	3.8	6.1	2.4	6.3	2.5	6.9	1.1	7.1	2.5
Trade[b]	15.5	4.3	18.7	7.1	15.2	8.6	15.9	8.6	20.3	11.5	22.6	9.7
Service	23.5	5.8	26.2	18.6	25.2	14.3	31.0	19.7	25.2	18.5	27.0	25.3
Total	100.0	100.0	100.0	100.0	100.0	100.0	100.0	100.0	100.0	100.0	100.0	100.0
N (in thousands)	20,700	968	22,315	1,930	18,850	914	19,100	1,580	2,554	649	2,316	738
Index of concentration	.16	.36	.14	.27	.05	.12	.07	.12	.09	.14	.08	.13
Index of dissimilarity	32.4		20.4		27.6		27.0		27.8		25.5	

[a]Figures for Germany exclude owners and self-employed.

[b]Figures for Switzerland include hotels and restaurants in this category.

Sources: Germany (endogenous population): *Yearbook of Labor Statistics* (Geneva: International Labour Office, 1970), p. 132, and 1982, p. 76; (foreign labor): Stephen Castles and Godula Kosack, *Immigration Workers and the Class Structure in Western Europe* (Oxford: Oxford University Press, 1973), pp. 72–73, and SOPEMI, *Continuous Reporting System on Migration* (Paris: OECD, 1982), p. 67. France (endogenous population): *Yearbook of Labour Statistics* (Geneva: International Labour Office, 1976), p. 132; (foreign labor): Michael J. Piore, *Birds of Passage* (London: Cambridge University Press, 1979), pp. 19–20, and SOPEMI, *Continuous Reporting System on Migration* (Paris: OECD, 1977), p. 19. Switzerland (endogenous population): *Yearbook of Labour Statistics* (Geneva: International Labour Office, 1975), p. 144, and 1982, p. 82; (foreign labor): Sashia Sassen-Koob, "The International Circulation of Resources and Development: The Case of Migrant Labor," *Development and Change* 9 (1978):509–45, and SOPEMI, *Continuous Reporting System on Migration* (Paris: OECD, 1982), p. 80.

tively dispersed across industries by 1972 and there was not much room left for change.

As noted earlier, change occurs in the industrial distribution of migrant (guest) workers to the extent that they become more dispersed and more integrated into the economic structure and come closer to having an industrial distribution similar to that of the host population. Nevertheless, the situation in Israel as measured by the index of dissimilarity exhibits by far the largest difference between foreign and local labor forces. This minimal incorporation may be a result of the unique situation whereby economic relations between Israel and residents of the administered territories are overshadowed by the broader Israeli-Arab conflict. A large part of Israel's manufacturing industry, for example, includes firms that produce "classified" items for defense from which nonresident Arabs are barred. Further, the period of contact in Israel has been relatively short, and an ongoing process may lead to further penetration of noncitizen Arabs into major economic sectors.

Noncitizen Arabs within a Comparative Framework

A key to understanding the disadvantages of noncitizen Arab workers appears to be their unique nonresident status. As a consequence of this status, workers cannot act freely in the labor market. As noted earlier, official work permits are required of noncitizen Arab workers employed in Israel, and shifting from one employer to another must first be approved by the Government Employment Service. Furthermore, nonresident status is inherently temporary. Although noncitizen Arab workers are permitted to organize, in effect they do not do so. They do not benefit from union protection and hence are a target for employer exploitation. The benefits to employers are not industry-specific. All sectors could and did reorganize, to one extent or another, to make use of the available cheap labor. At the same time, noncitizens lacked the resources to demand or compete for more rewarding jobs. Consequently, their occupational disadvantage has been extreme and has not improved over time.

It should be recalled that all countries that import labor have to some extent developed policies and regulations that control the entry, movement, and activities of guest (or migrant) labor. If we might generalize from the present analysis, the findings illustrate how the policies and regulations employed by a society constrain the labor market activities of foreign workers. The legal and political status of workers, it follows, is an important variable in determining the degree of occupational success and integration experienced by ethnic minorities.

By situating the discussion within a comparative framework, it is possible to gain greater insight into the experience of noncitizen Arabs in the Israeli market. This is not to say that the situation of noncitizen Arabs in Israel is identical to that of Turks in Germany or Italian workers in Switzerland. Nor is it suggested that the circumstances of migrant labor in the United States and in various European countries are the same. Differences exist, and important ones at that. We propose, however, that underlying labor market processes are sufficiently similar to render comparisons meaningful. In all cases migrant labor is generated by economic demand and is screened politically, resulting in a set of administrative regulations that limit the options of nonnationals and render them more vulnerable than the local labor force to economic exploitation. These elements are present in Israel as in other places. Our analysis indicated that to the extent that comparisons of labor market positions are possible, the situation of noncitizen Arabs in Israel is worse relative to that of nonnationals in other countries. The reason is a matter for speculation. That the situation of noncitizen Arabs is embedded in a broader national conflict and in many respects is involuntary may render them more vulnerable than other nonnationals. Further, noncitizen Arabs do not live in Israel and are isolated from all social institutions, which may facilitate their labor market exploitation more than is possible in most other circumstances. Hence, as long as Arabs from the administered territories continue to work within Israel, they may well be relegated to the lower rungs of the occupational ladder. In this respect, Israel manages to reap the benefits of employing foreign labor without experiencing the full social burden of incorporating them residentially and institutionally into the society.

7

Conclusion

Two decades have passed since residents of the West Bank and the Gaza Strip came under Israeli control. The circumstances that precipitated the contact were unique, of course, and embedded in the broader Israeli-Arab conflict still waiting to be resolved. Employment arrangements were thus part of the security and political measures adopted to enable "normal" life to resume. With time, employment of noncitizen Arabs in Israel became a central element of the economic life of residents of the administered territories and an enduring feature of the Israeli labor market. The entry of noncitizen Arabs into the Israeli market took place in specific industrial sectors that experienced labor shortages. These shortages were viewed as temporary difficulties that could be solved to the mutual benefit of both unemployed residents of the West Bank and the Gaza Strip and the industries in need of labor, at least until the final status of these territories was determined.

During the period of full employment, local workers in Israel took advantage of expanding opportunities in better-paying white-collar and technical occupations. Noncitizen Arab laborers were left with those jobs abandoned by others. Consequently, noncitizen Arab workers flowed into occupations throughout the economy, and their industrial distribution became less concentrated and more like that of the Israeli labor force. The dynamics in the occupational sphere, however, were different. Although noncitizen Arabs penetrated an increasing number of occupations over the years and some became more skilled and advanced on the occupational ladder, the overwhelming majority remained at the bottom of the hierarchy. So, although their wages, welfare, and social benefits improved, their subordinate position in the occupational structure relative to the local population remained unaltered.

The main goal of our investigation was to examine within a dynamic framework the integration of noncitizen Arabs and the impact they have had on the Israeli labor market. We undertook this task to assess a series of theoretical formulations on the process of ethnic stratification in the labor market. Subsequently, several conclusions have become readily apparent.

First, noncitizen Arabs have not found jobs across the occupational spectrum. Rather, they have concentrated at the bottom of the occupational ladder. Like other ethnic minorities and foreign labor, they tended to fill the low-status, least desirable, menial occupations. They have become the hewers of wood and drawers of water of Israeli society.

Second, it appears that an increase in participation of a subordinate ethnic minority in a labor market may well lead to its greater occupational subordination. The influx of minority workers increases the supply of cheap labor and thereby becomes an immediate target for economic exploitation and discrimination. Indeed, noncitizen Arabs have entered the Israeli labor market at the end of the occupational queue. Their dramatic influx explains, to some extent, why their average occupational position has worsened over time, both in absolute and relative terms.

Third, the occupational segregation of noncitizen Arabs and the decline in their occupational status are much more pronounced when one considers the structural shift of the occupational system. Jews (and local Arabs) have benefited greatly from occupational upgrading and consequently have enjoyed upward (structural) mobility. Noncitizen Arabs, on the contrary, have not benefited from such structural shifts. Apparently, minorities at the end of the occupational queue cannot take full advantage of structural changes. Moreover, their influx may well prompt upward occupational mobility for those at the top of the queue.

Fourth, entry of a subordinate ethnic minority into a labor market may have detrimental effects on the income level of some members of the superordinate group. Apparently, the concentration of noncitizen Arabs in lower-status occupations generated greater competition in these occupational labor markets. Consequently, this competition has led to a decline in the income level of Israeli incumbents still employed in these occupations.

Fifth, like other minority workers, not only have noncitizen Arabs been segregated to lower-status occupations, but their income has been considerably lower than that paid to other incumbents in these occupations. Nonetheless, their "human capital" and occupational distribution cannot fully account for their income subordination. Some of the income gap may well be explained by market discrimination. The unique status of noncitizen Arabs in Israeli society makes such economic discrimination more possible.

Sixth, our analysis clearly demonstrates that social and market conditions have governed, to a great extent, processes associated with the employment of noncitizen Arabs in Israel. Consequently, the phenomenon can be explained within the theoretical framework of ethnic stratification in the labor market. The conclusions thus should not be limited to Israel but generalized to other social contexts. Certain specific findings surely would be observed in societies other than Israel. Other conclusions are more general and were derived from the social and market conditions that govern the dynamics of stratification.

Indeed, our investigation focused exclusively on the labor market process. We are well aware that the issue has not been fully exhausted. There are several important issues that we did not investigate. Hence we cannot conclude this discussion without listing several important issues and questions that reach beyond our data.

One question our study did not answer, and that we did not have the data to examine, is whether and to what extent having a supply of cheap labor was detrimental to technological development, that is, whether there was less incentive to invest in long-range technological development because cheap labor was abundant. In the long run, a supply of cheap labor may suppress technological and economic progress. It is highly possible that this has been the case in Israel and in other societies that "import" and rely on cheap labor. There is scattered evidence that points toward such a possibility in Israel, though the issue has not been systematically studied.

It is not clear from our data the extent to which the segregation of noncitizen Arab workers in a few occupations has attached a negative connotation to these occupations. Nor is it clear whether such a connotation has prevented Jews from seeking employment or working in these occupations. Although we did not examine these possibilities, they are highly probable. In fact, the insight we have into Israeli society suggests, rather forcefully, that this is indeed the case.

Our data indicate that the integration of noncitizen Arabs into the Israeli economy has reshaped Israel's structure of inequality. The level of inequality has increased considerably since the influx of this subordinate ethnic group into the system. Their entry has made the overlap between ethnicity and class more pronounced and extreme. Sociological theory and research have long demonstrated that conflict is more likely in social systems characterized by high levels of inequality. The extent to which such inequality has increased ethnic antagonism, reshaped ethnic stereotypes, and affected political attitudes and behavior has yet to be answered. It is our hope that our study will stimulate further research that will provide systematic answers to these questions.

Appendixes

Appendix A
Labor Force and Income Surveys Used in the Study

The labor force survey covers all the permanent population of Israel aged fourteen and over, including potential immigrants and permanent residents staying abroad for a period of less than one year and excluding tourists and temporary residents. The survey is conducted four times a year. As part of the survey, an annual income survey is conducted in which one panel is interviewed in each quarter regarding its income in the previous twelve months. Since 1968, separate labor force surveys have been conducted in the West Bank and in the Gaza Strip. The content of the surveys changed somewhat over the years, and the samples grew considerably, as illustrated in table A.1 (detailed information regarding the surveys is given in Israel Central Bureau of Statistics Technical Reports).

TABLE A.1 Sample Sizes of the Surveys Used in the Analysis

Year	Labor Force Surveys[a] (Israel)	Income Surveys[b] (total)	Labor Force Surveys (administered territories)[a]
1969	6000	11,812	3900
1975	10,00	7449	6500
1981	12,000	6860	6100
1982	12,000	—	6100

[a]Households.
[b]Individuals.

DEFINITIONS

Employed persons: A person who worked for at least one hour in any work or gainful activity during the determinant week; a worker in a kibbutz (in service or in any other branch); an unpaid family member or an unpaid inmate of an institution who worked more than fifteen hours during the determinant week. Also included are persons temporarily absent from work who were not seeking other employment during the determinant week. Since 1967, Yeshiva students eighteen years and over who are actively employed in teaching are also treated as employed persons.

Employed persons are divided into three groups:

Full-time workers: Those who worked for at least thirty-five hours during the determinant week.

Part-time workers: Those who worked one to thirty-four hours (including preparation hours) during the determinant week.

Temporary absentees from work: Includes those temporarily absent from work during the determinant week because of sickness, holidays, service in the reserve army, strike, bad weather, temporary disruption (up to thirty days), and the like. Not included are absentees who sought other employment during their absence from work.

Unemployed: All those who did not work even one hour in the determinant week and who were actively seeking work in that week by virtue of being registered at the labor exchange of the Employment Service or at any other labor exchange, applying in person or writing, attempting to establish an independent business, or other acceptable means. Workers who were temporarily absent from work and seeking other work are also included.

The unemployed are divided into two groups:

Unemployed who worked in Israel during the twelve months prior to the determinant week.

Unemployed who have not worked in Israel for the last twelve months prior to the determinant week.

Not in civilian labor force: All persons aged fourteen years and over who were neither "employed" nor "unemployed" in the determinant week. This group includes students (excluding Yeshiva students aged eighteen and over actively engaged in teaching), housewives (who have not worked for even one hour outside their homes), persons incapacitated for work, pensioners and persons living on their income who have not worked for even one hour during the determinant week, servicemen in the armed forces (conscripted and regular army), unpaid family members, and inmates of institutions who worked less than fifteen hours per week.

Economic branch: Classification by economic branch is defined according to the type of establishment where the employed person worked. Employed persons are classified in the economic branch to which the establishment (or institution) in which they are employed belongs. The branch is determined by the product or main service of the establishment. Persons employed by establishments or institutions active in more than one branch (e.g., some textiles complexes or municipalities) will be classified by economic branch according to the branch of the department or division in which they are employed (a subsidiary unit of the establishment is not treated as a separate department). If the establishment is engaged in different but separate economic activities, the economic branch of the establishment will be determined according to the final product.

Occupation: Occupation refers to the kind of work the employed person actually performs without regard to the profession for which he is qualified. The classification is based on the International Standard Classification of Occupations, which was prepared by the International Labour Organization and was adapted to the requirements of Israel's economy.

Appendix B

Matching of Three-digit Occupational Categories from the Revised Classification with Two-digit Categories from the Old Classification and Their Socioeconomic Scores

Occupational Title	Detailed Occupations	Status Score
Class 0: Scientific and academic professionals		
00 Engineers, architects, etc.	020 Architects and town planners	
	021 Civil engineers	
	022 Electrical and electronics engineers	
	023 Mechanical engineers	
	024 Aeronautical engineers	86
	026 Metallurgical engineers	
	027 Industrial and methods engineers	
	028 Engineers (n.e.c.)[a]	
	02v Engineers (n.s.)[b]	
	170 Surveyors	
	171 Technicians[c]—civil engineering	
	172 Technicians[c]—electrical and electronics engineering	
	173 Technicians[c]—mechanical engineering	
	174 Technicians[c]—chemical engineering, metallurgy, mining engineering, metal and petroleum processings engineer	56
	175 Draughtsmen	
	176 Production and management technicians	
	178 Technicians[c] (n.e.c.)	
	17v Technicians[c] (n.s.)	
	180 System analysts	
	181 Programmers	66
	1v Technicians (n.s.)	

Source: Israel Central Bureau of Statistics, *Census of Population and Housing, 1972, Labour Force,* Pt. II, 1979.

[a]No exact classification.

[b]Not specified.

[c]Includes practical engineers.

01 Chemists, physicists, geologists, biologists, veterinarians, agronomists and other workers in natural and life sciences	000 Biologists and related scientists 001 Pharmacologists and related scientists 002 Biochemists 003 Agronomists 00v Academic workers in life sciences (n.s.)	} 75
	010 Chemists 011 Physicists 012 Academic workers in natural sciences (n.e.c.) 01v Academic workers in natural sciences (n.s.)	} 78
	025 Chemical engineers	} 86
	041 Veterinarians	} 75
	16v Natural sciences technicians (n.s.)	} 60
02 Medical doctors and dental surgeons	030 Medical doctors 031 Dentists	} 87
03 Nurses and midwives	150 Qualified nurses 151 Practical nurses and practical midwives	} 51
04 Medical technicians and workers in paramedical professions (n.e.c. and n.s.)	240 Pharmacists	} 87
	153 Optometrists 154 Therapists 155 Other medical technicians 15v Workers in paramedical professions 158 Other workers in paramedical professions (n.s.)	} 51
	032 Practical dentists	} 75
	583 Dental assistants	} 31
05 Teachers	080 Higher education -08v teachers in life and natural sciences, engineering, medicine, law, social sciences, and humanities, and others in higher education institutions 090 Headmasters in postsecondary and postprimary educational institutions	} 86

091 Inspectors of postsecondary
     and postprimary educational
     institutions
092 Teachers in postsecondary
     educational institutions
093 Teachers in postprimary
     educational institutions   } 81
094 Heads and teachers in
     religious academies
     (Yeshivot) (postsecondary)
095 Vocational instructors

100 Headmasters in secondary
     and primary schools
101 Inspectors of secondary
     schools, primary schools,
     kindergartens, etc.
102 Secondary school teachers
103 Primary school teachers
104 Kindergarten teachers   } 71
105 Special education teachers
107 Teachers in courses for arts
     and crafts, driving, etc.
108 Other teachers in various
     institutions
10v Teachers (n.s.)

582 Kindergarten assistants   } 31

141 Youth instructors   } 52

06 Workers in religion	120 Workers in the Jewish religion	
	121 Rabbis	
	123 Workers in the Moslem religion	} 50
	124 Workers in the Christian religion	
	128 Workers in other religions (n.e.c.)	

07 Judges and jurists	050 Judges	
	051 Religious court judges	
	052 Lawyers	} 83
	058 Jurists (n.e.c.)	
	123 Pleaders in religious courts (Jewish)	} 50

08 Authors, artists, and related occupations	130 Authors and journalists 131 Sculptors, painters, and related artists 132 Workers in applied art 134 Composers, musicians, and related occupations 135 Actors and dancers 136 Stage directors and film producers	} 57
09 Academic workers in humanities and social sciences	100 Accountants 111 Cost accountants	} 75
	140 Social workers	} 60
	070 Academic workers in humanities 071 Academic workers in Jewish studies 072 Translators 07v Academic workers in humanities (n.s.)	} 74
	060 Statisticians 061 Mathematicians and actuaries 062 Economists 063 Psychologists 064 Sociologists and other workers in social sciences 06v Academic workers in social sciences (n.s.)	} 52

*Class 1: Managers/
administrators and clerical
workers*

10 Managers of governmental and municipal and public institutions	200 Members of the legislative and executive authorities (central government) 201 Members of the legislative and executive authorities (local government)	} 59
	210 Managers-administrators in governmental and municipal services and national institutions	} 68

220 Managers of governmental, municipal, and public professional units for natural sciences, life sciences, and medicine
221 Managers of governmental, municipal, and public professional units for engineering } 82

230 Managers of governmental, municipal, and public professional (institutions and institutes) units for humanities and social sciences
231 Managers of governmental, municipal, and public professional (institutions and institutes) units for law } 76

351 Post office branch managers } 60

300 Departmental managers and clerical supervisors in government service } 48

| 11–15 Managers in industry | 240 General managers
241 Production managers
242 Bank and insurance company branch managers
243 General contractors
244 Hotel and other guest house managers
248 Managers (n.e.c.)
2vv Managers (n.s.) | } 76 |

421 Subagency, department store, and supermarket managers } 60

301 Clerical supervisors
304 Clerical supervisors (n.s.) } 50

| 16 Bookkeepers and cashiers | 310 Bookkeepers
311 Treasurers
312 Cashiers and other accountant clerks | } 44 |

| 17 Secretaries, typists, and stenographers | 320 Secretaries, typists, and stenographers | } 37 |

| 18 Office equipment operators | 321 Card-punching machine operators
322 Bookkeeping machine operators | } 37 |

	837 Automatic data-processing machine operators	} 40
19 Storekeepers and other clerical workers (n.e.c. and n.s.)	318 Accounts clerks (n.e.c.) 31v Accounts (n.s.) 330 Storekeepers	} 44
	331 Filing clerks 370 Office clerks (general)	} 38
	380 Receptionists 381 Library clerks 388 Clerks (n.e.c.) 3vv Clerks (n.s.)	} 40

Class 2: Merchants, brokers, and agents

20 Merchants, agents, and salesmen	400 Wholesalers (working proprietors)	} 56
21 Retailers (working proprietors)	410 Retailers (working proprietors) 411 Fixed stall proprietors (not for sale of food products) 412 Retail station proprietors	} 39
22 Insurance agents, stockbrokers, appraisers, customs agents, travel agents, and auctioneers	420 Buyers and sales supervisors 422 Technical sales agents and technical sales advisers	} 50
	430 Insurance agents 431 Estate agents and intermediaries 432 Stockbrokers and stockjobbers 433 Travel agents 435 Appraisers and auctioneers 436 Customs agents	} 52
23 Agents and commercial travelers	423 Commercial travelers and factory agents	} 50
	434 Advertising agents and ticket sales agents 438 Agents (n.e.c.)	} 32
24 Salesmen	440 Salesmen and shop assistants 441 Petrol pump attendants	} 29
25 Milkmen, ice vendors, kerosene vendors, and newspaper distributors	450 Milkmen, ice vendors, and kerosene vendors	} 21
26 Peddlers and mobile stall proprietors	451 Peddlers and mobile stall proprietors	} 21

	452 Lottery ticket vendors	
	503 Working proprietors in catering services: stalls for sale of food items, kiosks	} 37

Class 3 Farmers, fishers, and related workers

30 Farm workers in more than one agricultural branch	607 Farmers working in more than one agricultural branch 60v Farmers working their own farms	} 30
	61v Branch coordinators and supervisors (n.s.)	} 21
	627 Skilled workers in more than one agricultural branch 62v Skilled farm workers (n.s.) 6vv Farmers (n.s.)	} 45
31 Cattle farm workers	603 Cattle farmers	} 30
	614 Cattle, sheep, and goat branch coordinators and supervisors	} 45
	623 Skilled cattle workers	} 21
32 Poultry branch workers	605 Poultry farmers	} 30
	615 Poultry branch coordinators and supervisors	} 45
	625 Skilled poultry workers	} 21
34 Fisheries branch workers	616 Fisheries branch coordinators and supervisors	} 45
35 Livestock branch workers (n.e.c.)	606 Other livestock farmers	} 30
	610 Farm coordinators (general)	} 45
	626 Skilled livestock workers 628 Skilled farm workers (n.e.c.)	} 28
	192 Agricultural instructors (not in educational institutions)	} 60
36 Farm machinery operators	640 Farm machinery operators	} 28
37 Field crop and industry workers, vegetable, orchard (including citrus grove), flower, and nursery branch workers (not including pickers and caretakers)	600 Field crop and vegetable farmers 601 Flower and nursery farmers 602 Orchard (including citrus grove) farmers	} 30

	611 Field crop and vegetable branch coordinators and supervisors	
	612 Flower and nursery branch coordinators and supervisors	} 45
	613 Orchard (including citrus grove) branch coordinators and supervisors	
	620 Skilled field crop and vegetable workers	
	621 Skilled flower and nursery workers	} 21
	622 Skilled plantation workers	
	650 Shift foremen in packing house and shift foremen in packing and sorting house	
	651 Machine operators, fork-lift truck operators, and packing and sorting house maintenance men	
	652 Unskilled workers in sorting, handling, washing, waxing, and packing fruit and vegetables	} 21
	65v Packing and sorting house workers (n.s.)	
104 Unskilled agricultural workers	660 Forestry workers	
	661 Citrus fruit pickers	
	662 Pickers and gatherers of other crops	} 12
	663 Unskilled workers in land reclamation	
	66v Unskilled agricultural workers (n.s.)	

Class 4 Transport workers and communications occupations

40 Ships' officers	190 Ships' officers	} 60
41 Deck and bridge	870 Deck and bridge ratings	} 42
42 Aircraft officers	191 Aircraft officers	} 60
43 Railway station masters	350 Railway station masters	} 30
	361 Passenger train ticket inspectors	} 42
	872 Railway engine drivers and other railway workers	} 48

44 Motor bus drivers	880 Motor bus drivers 881 Semitrailer and trailer lorry drivers 883 Special motor vehicle drivers 88v Drivers (n.s.)	} 35
45 Taxi drivers	882 Taxi drivers 884 Drivers of passenger motor vehicles (except motor buses and taxis)	} 35
46 Commercial drivers	885 Drivers of other goods-transporting motor vehicles 886 Drivers of commercial vans	} 35
47 Telephone, telegraph, and radio operators	340 Telephone and telegraph operators 341 Radio-telephone operators	} 37
48 Postmen and messengers	362 Postmen 363 Messengers	} 30
49 Supervisors in transport and communications	352 Postal workers' supervisors 358 Transport and communications supervisors 35v Transport and communications supervisors (n.s.)	} 30
	360 Bus inspectors and conductors	} 48

Class 5: Excavation, building, and mine workers

51 Construction workers	852 Tile setters and mosaic panel workers 853 Plasterers 854 Insulators 857 Concrete pourers 858 Prefabricated structure assemblers 859 Stonemasons, stonecutters, and other building workers (n.e.c.)	} 33
52 Painters and whitewashers	891 Building painters and whitewashers 898 Painters (n.e.c.)	} 30
53 Glaziers	855 Glaziers	} 33
54 Electric power, telephone, and telegraph linemen	746 Electric power, telephone, and telegraph linemen	} 38

55 Plumbers	731 Plumbers	
	732 Sewage and drainage pipe fitters	} 33
56 Excavating and road construction machine operators	863 Excavating, building, and road construction machine operators	
	868 Excavating, building, and road construction machine operators (n.e.c.)	} 39
	981 Road-surface layers, tar spreaders, and pavers	} 16
58 Miners	841 Miners and quarrymen	
	842 Quarrying machine operators	} 37
	843 Drillers and related workers	
59 Unskilled workers (n.e.c.)	980 Unskilled workers in land reclamation	} 16
	990 Unskilled construction workers (n.s.)	} 19

Class 6–8: Workers in crafts and manufacturing

60 Knitting workers	792 Spinners and winders	
	793 Knitting machine setters	
	794 Weavers	} 26
	795 Knitters	
61 Bleachers, dyers	791 Fiber preparers	
	796 Textile bleachers, dyers, and finishers	} 26
	798 Textile processing workers (n.e.c.)	
62 Dressmakers and tailors	801 Dressmakers and tailors (made-to-measure garments)	
	805 Tailors (ready-to-wear garments)	} 24
	80v Tailors and dressmakers (n.s.)	
63 Fur tailors	802 Fur tailors	
	803 Hatmakers and milliners	
	804 Cloth and leather garment pattern makers, markers, and cutters	} 24
	806 Tailors (leather garments)	
	807 Embroiderers	
64 Upholsterers	808 Upholsterers	} 24

65 Shoe cutters, shoe sewers, and other shoe part makers	812 Shoe repairers and shoemakers 813 Shoe cutters, shoe sewers, and other shoe part makers 818 Workers in leather goods and manufacture (n.e.c.) 81v Leather workers (n.s.)	} 23
66 Skilled and semiskilled workers in the metal industry	701 Metal casters 702 Metal rolling mill workers 703 Electroplaters and hot-dip platers 708 Metal processors (n.e.c.) 70v Metal processors (n.s.)	} 35
	711 Workers in metal shavings 712 Sheet-metal workers 713 Welders and flame cutters 714 Metal structure assemblers and boilermakers 715 Toolmakers 716 Locksmiths (general) 717 Blacksmiths 718 Sheet-metal workers, welders, blacksmiths, and workers in finished metal products (n.e.c.) 71v Workers in manufacture and processing of finished metal	} 34
	721 Engine assemblers and installers 722 Assemblers and repairers of machinery (all types) 723 Assemblers of motor vehicles (all types) 724 Locksmiths and machinery repairers	} 35
69 Vehicle repairers	725 Vehicle repairers (all types) and mechanics (n.s.)	} 35
	892 Motor vehicle painters	} 30
70 Cabinetmakers	781 Cabinetmakers 782 Woodworking machine operators 788 Woodworkers, carpenters, and related occupations (n.e.c.) 78v Woodworkers and carpenters (n.s.)	} 28

71 Unskilled workers in basketry products	971 Unskilled workers in basketry products	} 27
72 Diamond polishers	761 Diamond polishers 762 Other diamond workers 76v Diamond workers (n.s.)	} 36
73 Opticians	152 Opticians	} 51
74 Watchmakers	751 Watchmakers 752 Assemblers and repairers of precision instruments 753 Silversmiths and goldsmiths	} 36
	832 Dental technicians	} 40
76 Electricians and electrical equipment operators	741 Assemblers and repairers of electrical and electronic equipment 742 Manufacturers, assemblers, and repairers of radio and television equipment and loudspeakers 743 Assemblers and repairers of electronic equipment 745 Electricians and electrical equipment operators 747 Telephone and telegraph assemblers and repairers 748 Building electricians 74v Electricians (n.s.)	} 38
78 Bookbinders	821 Printing compositors and typesetters 822 Printing pressmen, platers, and lithographers 823 Printing engravers (except photoengravers) 824 Zincographers and draughtsmen 825 Bookbinders 828 Printing workers (n.e.c.) 82v Printing workers (n.s.)	} 37
79 Craftsmen	833 Ceramic workers 834 Glass workers	} 40
80 Unskilled workers in rubber products manufacture	920 Unskilled workers in typemaking 921 Unskilled workers in rubber products manufacture	} 38

81 Workers in oil and chemical processing

910 Unskilled workers in refining petroleum and petroleum products
911 Cookers and roasters and other workers in chemical processing and in nonmetallic mineral production
912 Unskilled workers in crushing, grinding, and rolling chemicals, plastic, and rubber materials
913 Paper-pulp preparers
914 Paper-working workers
915 Workers in sugar refining and in edible oil and alcoholic beverages manufacture
918 Unskilled workers in chemical processing (n.e.c.)
91v Unskilled workers in chemical processing (n.s.)

} 36

831 Skilled workers in chemical production processing

} 40

970 Unskilled workers in manufacture of paper products

} 27

---

82 Millers

771 Bakers
772 Skilled workers in food production and preservation
773 Skilled workers in dairies and milk production
774 Butchers and slaughterers
775 Millers
776 Pastry makers
778 Other skilled workers in processing food, beverages, and tobacco

} 28

	930 Unskilled baking workers	
	931 Unskilled cake-baking workers	
	932 Unskilled workers in processing hard and soft drinks	
	934 Unskilled workers in meat processing and meat products	} 24
	935 Unskilled dairy workers	
	938 Unskilled workers in food and beverage manufacture (n.e.c. and n.s.)	
83 Tanners and pelt dressers	811 Tanners and pelt dressers	} 23
85 Engine and pump operators and steam boiler firemen	836 Steam boiler firemen	} 40
	940 Engine and pump operators	
	941 Oilers and greasers	} 34
	861 Wiremen and cablemen	
	862 Crane and elevator operators	} 39
86 Packers	950 Industrial packers	
	951 Labelers and related occupations	} 22
87 Dockers and lightermen	901 Dockers and lightermen	
	902 Porters	} 21
89 Other workers in manufacturing	826 Photographic dark-room workers	} 37
	835 Musical instrument makers	} 40
	960 Workers in manufacture of nonmetallic mineral products	} 25
	972 Unskilled workers in manufacture of miscellaneous products (n.e.c.)	} 27
Class A: Workers in sports recreation and entertainment 90 Policemen and police detectives	570 Policemen and police detectives	
	571 Firemen	
	572 Prison guards	} 31
	573 Watchmen and guardsmen	
	578 Other security workers	

91 Service workers	540 Charworkers and housemaids 541 Cooks (in private service) 542 Nursemaids (unqualified)	} 19
	594 Kitchen workers in institutions (not cooks)	} 13
92 Workers in food and lodging services	500 Working proprietors in lodging services 501 Working proprietors in catering services: reception halls and restaurants 502 Working proprietors in catering services: stalls for sale of food items	} 37
	510 Head cooks and cooks	} 25
	520 Waiters 521 Barmen 522 Stewards	} 28
	530 Housekeepers 531 Room cleaners and chambermaids	} 32
	580 Air stewards	} 31
93 Janitors and cleaners	591 Janitors and caretakers 592 Cleaners in institutions 593 Street cleaners	} 13
94 Hairdressers and beauticians	560 Ladies' hairdressers 561 Mens' hairdressers and hairdressers (n.s.) 562 Beauticians	} 21
95 Dry cleaners and garment dyers	550 Laundry proprietors 551 Dry cleaners and garment dyers 552 Launderers	} 24
96 Athletes and entertainers	198 Free professionals, technicians, and related occupations (n.e.c.)	} 60
	138 Entertainment workers (n.e.c.)	} 57
97 Photographers	133 Photographers	} 57
98 Undertakers	590 Undertakers	} 13
99 Guides	581 Guides and information guides	} 13
	598 Service workers (n.e.c.)	} 31

	442 Male and female fashion models	} 29
109 Unskilled industrial workers (n.s.)	191 Unskilled industrial workers (n.s.)	} 19
	99v Unskilled workers (n.s.)	} 19

References

Adler, I., and R. W. Hodge
    1983   Ethnicity and the process of status attainment. *Israel social science research* 1:5–23.

Allport, G. W.
    1954   *The nature of prejudice*. Boston: Beacon Press.

Almquist, E. M.
    1975   Untangling the effects of race and sex: The disadvantaged status of black women. *Social science quarterly* 56:129–42.

Amir, S.
    1978a   The employment of residents of the administered territories in Israel. *Labour and national insurance* 30:79–80 (Hebrew).
    1978b   A decade of activities in the sphere of labour and employment in the administered territories, 1967–1977. *Labour and national insurance* 30:297–301 (Hebrew).
    1985   *Labour and employment in Judea, Samaria, and the Gaza District*. Jerusalem: State of Israel, Ministry of Labour and Social Affairs.

Baron, H. M.
    1973   Racial domination in advanced capitalism: A theory of nationalism. In *Labor market segmentation*, edited by R. C. Edwards, M. R. Reich, and D. M. Gordon, 173–216. Lexington, Mass.: D. C. Heath.

Beck, E. M.
    1980   Discrimination and white economic loss: A time series examination of the radical model. *Social forces* 59:148–68.

Blalock, H. M.
    1967   *Toward a theory of minority group relations*. New York: John Wiley and Sons.

Blau, P. M., and O. D. Duncan
    1967   *The American occupational structure*. New York: John Wiley and Sons.

Böhning, W. R.
    1972   *The migration of workers in the United Kingdom and the European community*. London: Oxford University Press.
    1984   *Studies in international labour migration*. New York: St. Martin's.

Bohrnstedt, G. W.
    1969   Observation in the measurement of change. In *Sociological methodology*, edited by E. F. Borgata, 113–33. San Francisco: Jossey-Bass.

Bonacich, E.
    1972   A theory of ethnic antagonism: The split labor market. *American sociological review* 37:547–59.
    1976   Advanced capitalism and black-white race relations in the United States: A split labor market interpretation. *American sociological review* 41:34–51.

Bovenkerk, F.
    1979   The Netherlands. In *International labor migration in Europe*, edited by R. E. Krane, 118–32. New York: Praeger.

Boyd, M., D. L. Featherman, and J. Matras
    1980   Status attainment of immigrants, and immigrant origin groups in the United States, Canada, and Israel. *Comparative social research* 3:199–228.

Broom, L., and N. Glenn
    1965   *Transformation of the Negro American*. New York: Harper & Row.

Brown, P. G., and H. Shue
    1983   *The border that joins: Mexican migrants and U.S. responsibility*. Totowa, N.J.: Rowman and Littlefield.

Castells, M.
    1978   Immigrant workers and class struggles in advanced capitalism: The Western European experience. *Politics and society* 5:33–66.

Castles, S., and G. Kosack
    1973   *Immigrant workers and class structure in Western Europe*. London: Oxford University Press.

Castles, S., with H. Booth and T. Wallace
  1984   *Here for good: Western Europe's new ethnic minorities.* London: Pluto Press.

Cutright, P.
  1965   Negro subordination and white gains. *American sociological review* 30:110–12.

Duncan, O. D.
  1966   Methodological issues in the analysis of social mobility. In *Social structure and mobility in economic development*, edited by N. J. Smelser and S. M. Lipset, 51–97. Chicago: Aldine.
  1968   Inheritance of poverty or inheritance of race? In *On understanding poverty: Perspectives from the social sciences*, edited by D. P. Moynihan, 85–110. New York: Basic Books.

Duncan, O. D., D. L. Featherman, and B. Duncan
  1972   *Socioeconomic background and achievement.* New York: Seminar Press.

Eisenstadt, S. N.
  1954   *The absorption of immigrants.* London: Routledge and Kegan Paul.
  1967   *Israeli society.* London: Weidenfeld and Nicholson.

Featherman, D. L., and R. M. Hauser
  1976   Changes in socioeconomic stratification of the races, 1962–1973. *American journal of sociology* 82:621–51.

Fischer, C.
  1975   Toward a subcultural theory of urbanism. *American journal of sociology* 80:1319–51.

Fossett, M.
  1984   City differences in racial occupational differentiation: A note in the use of odds ratios. *Demography* 21:655–66.

Fossett, M., and G. Swicegood
  1982   Racial occupational inequality. *American sociological review* 47:631–89.

Frazier, E.
  1951   The Negro's vested interest in segregation. In *Race, prejudice, and discrimination*, edited by A. Rose, 332–39. New York: Knopf.

Frisbie, W. P., and L. Neidert
  1977   Inequality and the relative size of minority populations. A comparative analysis. *American journal of sociology* 32:1007–30.

Gibbs, J. P., and W. T. Martin
  1962 Urbanization, technology, and the division of labor: International patterns. *American sociological review* 27:607–27.

Glenn, N. D.
  1963 Occupational benefits to whites of the subordination of Negroes. *American sociological review* 28:443–48.
  1964 The relative size of the Negro population and Negro occupational status. *Social forces* 43:42–49.
  1966 White gains from Negro subordination. *Social problems* 14:159–78.

Goldthorpe, J.
  1980 *Social mobility and class structure in modern Britain*. Oxford: Clarendon Press.

Goodman, L.
  1972 A general model for the analysis of surveys. *American journal of sociology* 77:1035–86.

Gorz, A.
  1970 Immigrant labour. *New Left review* 61:28–31.

Grusky, D. B., and R. M. Hauser
  1984 Comparative social mobility revisited: Models of convergence and divergence in sixteen countries. *American sociological review* 49:19–38.

Hartman, M., and H. Eilon
  1975 Ethnicity and class in Israel. *Megamot* 21:129–39 (Hebrew).

Hauser, R. M., P. J. Dickinson, H. P. Travis, and J. H. Koffel
  1975 Structural changes in occupational mobility among men in the United States. *American sociological review* 40:585–98.

Hauser, R. M., and D. L. Featherman
  1977 *The process of stratification: Trends and analysis*. New York: Academic Press.

Hazelrigg, L. E., and M. A. Garnier
  1976 Occupational mobility in industrialized societies: A comparable analysis of differential access to occupational ranks in seventeen countries. *American sociological review* 41:498–511.

Hechter, M.
  1975 *Internal colonialism*. London: Routledge and Kegan Paul.

Heise, D. R.
  1970 Causal inference from panel data. In *Sociological methodology*, edited by E. F. Bergatta and G. W. Bohrnstedt, 3–27. San Francisco: Jossey-Bass.

Hodge, R. W.
    1973   Toward a theory of racial differences in employment. *Social forces* 52:16–31.

Hodge, R. W., and P. Hodge
    1965   Occupational assimilation as a competitive process. *American journal of sociology* 70:249–64.
    1966   Comment. *American journal of sociology* 72:286–89.

Hoffman-Nowotny, H.-J., and M. Killias
    1979   Switzerland. In *International migration in Europe*, edited by R. E. Krane, 45–62. New York: Praeger.

Hout, M.
    1984   Occupational mobility of black men. *American sociological review* 49:308–22.

Hudson, R., and R. L. Kaufman
    1982   Economic dualism: A critical review. *American sociological review* 47:727–39.

Iams, H., and A. Thornton
    1975   Decomposition of differences: A cautionary note. *Sociological methods and research* 3:341–52.

Kaufman, R. L.
    1983   A structural decomposition of black-white earning differentials. *American journal of sociology* 89:585–611.

Kaufman, R. L., and S. Spilerman
    1982   The age structures of occupations and jobs. *American journal of sociology* 87:827–51.

Kessler, R. C., and D. F. Greenberg
    1981   *Linear panel analysis*. New York: Academic Press.

Knoke, D., and P. J. Burke
    1980   *Log-linear models*. Beverly Hills, Calif.: Sage.

Kraus, V.
    1982   Ethnic origin as hierarchical dimension of social status and its correlates. *Sociology and social research* 66:252–66.

Labovitz, S., and R. Hagedorn
    1975   A structural-behavioral theory of intergroup antagonism. *Social forces* 53:444–48.

LaGory, M., and R. J. Magnani
    1979   Structural correlates of black-white occupational differentiation: Will U.S. regional differences in status remain? *Social problems* 27:157–69.

Laor, M.
1986 *Employment of residents from the administered territories employed in Israel*. Tel Aviv: Histadrut, Economic and Social Research Institute (Hebrew).

Lewin-Epstein, N.
1986 Effects of residential segregation and neighborhood opportunity structure on the employment of black and white youth. *Sociological quarterly* 27:559–70.

Lewin-Epstein N., and M. Semyonov
1984 Occupational change in Israel: Bringing the labor market back in. *Israel social science research* 2(2):3–18.

Lewis, W. A.
1985 *Racial conflict and economic development*. Cambridge and London: Harvard University Press.

Lieberson, S.
1970 Stratification and ethnic groups. *Sociological inquiry* 40:172–81.
1975 Rank sum comparison between groups. In *Sociological methodology*, edited by D. Heise, 276–91. San Francisco: Jossey-Bass.
1980 *A piece of the pie*. Berkeley: University of California Press.

Lieberson, S., and Fuguitt, G. V.
1967 Negro occupational differences in the absence of discrimination. *American journal of sociology* 73:188–200.

Light, I.
1972 *Ethnic enterprise in America*. Berkeley: University of California Press.
1981 Ethnic succession. In *Ethnic change*, edited by C. F. Keyes, 54–81. Seattle: University of Washington Press.
1984 Immigrant and ethnic enterprise in North America. *Ethnic and racial studies* 7:195–216.

Martin, W. G., and D. L. Poston, Jr.
1972 The occupational composition of white females: Sexism, racism and occupational differentiation. *Social forces* 50:349–55.

Matras, J.
1980 Comparative social mobility. *Annual review of sociology* 6:401–31.

Matras, J., and D. Weintraub
1976 Ethnic and other primordial differentials in intergenerational mobility in Israel. Paper presented at the Stratifi-

cation and Mobility Seminar of the International Sociological Association, Jerusalem, Israel.

McClendon, M. J.
1977 Structural and exchange components of vertical mobility. *American sociological review* 42:56–74.

McFarland, D.
1969 Measuring the permeability of occupational structures: An information-theoretic approach. *American journal of sociology* 75:41–61.

Murphy, R.
1985 Exploitation or exclusion? *Sociology* 19:225–43.

Nahon, Y.
1984 *Trends in occupational status—the ethnic dimension*. Jerusalem: Institute for Israel Studies (Hebrew).

Niemi, A. W., Jr.
1974 Wage discrimination against Negroes and Puerto Ricans in the New York SMSA: An assessment of educational and occupational differences. *Social science quarterly* 55:112–20.

Oz, A.
1983 *In the land of Israel*. San Diego: Harcourt Brace Jovanovich.

Park, R. E.
1952 *Human communities*. Glencoe, Ill.: Free Press.

Parkin, F.
1979 *Marxism and class theory: A bourgeois critique*. New York: Columbia University Press.

Peres, Y.
1971 Ethnic relations in Israel. *American journal of sociology* 76:1031–41.
1976 *Ethnic relations in Israel*. Tel Aviv: Sifriat Hapoalim (Hebrew).

Piore, M. J.
1979 *Birds of passage*. Cambridge: Cambridge University Press.

Pollard, S.
1979 The rise of service industries and white-collar employment. In *Post-industrial society*, edited by B. Gustofson, 17–43. New York: St. Martin's.

Portes, A.
1981 Modes of structural incorporation and present theories of labor migration. In *Global trends in migration: Theory and*

research on international population movements, edited by M. M. Kritz, C. B. Keely, and S. M. Tomas, 279–97. New York: Center for Migration Studies.

Power, J.
1979   *Migrant workers in Western Europe and the United States.* Oxford: Pergamon Press.

Reich, M.
1971   The economics of racism. In *Problems in political economy: An urban perspective*, edited by D. M. Gordon, 107–13. Lexington, Mass.: D. C. Heath.

Reimann, H., and H. Reimann
1979   Federal Republic of Germany. In *International labor migration in Europe*, edited by R. E. Krane, 68–87. New York: Praeger.

Reimers, C. W.
1984   Sources of family income among Hispanics, blacks, and white non-Hispanics. *American journal of sociology* 89:889–903.

Rekhes, E.
1975   Labourers from the administered territories working in Israel. Tel Aviv: Tel Aviv University. Mimeo.

Rex, J.
1979   Race relations theory and the study of migration to advanced industrial societies. In *Problems in international comparative research in the social sciences*, edited by B. F. Geyer and R. Jwekorich, 11–22. Oxford: Pergamon Press.

Robinson, R. V.
1984   Structural change and class mobility in capitalist societies. *Social forces* 63:51–71.

Rogers, R., ed.
1985   *Guests come to stay: The effects of European labor migration on sending and receiving countries.* Boulder, Col.: Westview Press.

Semyonov, M., and R. I. Scott
1983   Industrial shifts, female employment and occupational differentiation: A dynamic model for American cities, 1960–1970. *Demography* 20:163–76.

Semyonov, M., D. R. Hoyt, and R. I. Scott
1984   Place, race, and differential occupational opportunities. *Demography* 21:258–70.

Semyonov, M., and A. Tyree
  1981 Community segregation and the costs of ethnic subordination. *Social forces* 59:649–86.

Shalev, M.
  1986 Winking an eye at cheap Arab labour. *Jerusalem Post*, January 7, p. 8.

Shavit, Y.
  1984 Tracking and ethnicity in Israeli secondary education. *American sociological review* 49:210–21.

Shibutani, T., and K. M. Kawn
  1986 *Ethnic stratification: A comparative approach*. New York: Macmillan.

Shtendel, U.
  1971 *The minorities in Israel*. Jerusalem: Merkaz Ha'asbarah (Hebrew).

Shuval, J. T.
  1963 *Immigrants on the threshold*. New York: Atherton.

Siegel, P. M.
  1965 On the cost of being a Negro. *Sociological inquiry* 35:41–57.

Simkus, A.
  1984 Structural transformation and social mobility: Hungary 1938–1973. *American sociological review* 49:291–307.

Simon, R. J.
  1978 *Continuity and change: A study of two ethnic communities in Israel*. Cambridge: Cambridge University Press.

Simpson, I. H., R. L. Simpson, M. Evers, and S. S. Pass
  1982 Occupational recruitment, retention, and labor force cohort representation. *American journal of sociology* 87:1287–313.

Smooha, S.
  1978 *Israel: Pluralism and conflict*. Berkeley: University of California Press.

Smooha, S., and V. Kraus
  1985 Ethnicity as a factor in status attainment in Israel. *Research in social stratification and mobility* 4:151–75.

Smooha, S., and Y. Peres
  1976 The dynamics of ethnic inequalities: The case of Israel. *Social dynamics* 1:63–79.

Snyder, D., and P. M. Hudis
  1976 Occupational income and the effects of minority competition and segregation: A reanalysis and some new evidence. *American sociological review* 41:209–34.

Sorenson, A. B.
   1975   Models of social mobility. *Social science research* 4:65–92.

Spilerman, S.
   1977   Careers, labor market structure and socioeconomic achievement. *American journal of sociology* 83:551–93.

Spilerman, S., and R. E. Miller
   1977   City nondifference revisited. *American sociological review* 42:979–83.

Stolzenberg, R. M.
   1975a   Education, occupation and wage differences between white and black men. *American journal of sociology* 81:299–323.

   1975b   Occupations, labor markets and process of wage attainment. *American sociological review* 40:645–55.

Stolzenberg, R. M., and R. J. D'Amico
   1977   City differences and nondifferences in the effect of race and sex on occupational distribution. *American sociological review* 42:937–50.

Sullivan, T. A.
   1978   *Marginal workers, marginal jobs*. Austin and London: University of Texas Press.

Szymanski, A.
   1976   Racial discrimination and white gain. *American sociological review* 41:403–14.

Taeuber, A. F., K. E. Taeuber, and G. C. Cain
   1966   Occupational assimilation and the competition process: A reanalysis. *American journal of sociology* 72:273–85.

Taeuber, K. E., and Taeuber, A. F.
   1965   *Negroes in cities*. Chicago: Aldine.

Thurow, L. C.
   1975   *Generating inequality: Mechanisms of distribution in the U.S. economy*. New York: Basic Books.

Tyree, A.
   1981   Occupational socioeconomic status, ethnicity and sex in Israel: Consideration in scale construction. *Megamot* 27:7–21 (Hebrew).

Tyree, A., M. Semyonov, and R. W. Hodge
   1979   Gaps and glissandos: Inequality, economic development, and social mobility in twenty-four countries. *American sociological review* 44:410–24.

Upton, G. J. G.
   1978   *The analysis of cross-tabulated data*. Chichester: Basic Books.

Villemez, W. J.
    1978   Black subordination and white economic well-being. *American sociological review* 43:772–76.

Wilcox, J., and W. C. Roof
    1978   Percent black and black-white status inequality: Southern versus non-southern patterns. *Social science quarterly* 59:422–34.

Williams, R. M.
    1947   *The reduction of intergroup tensions*. New York: Social Science Research Council.

Yuchtman, E., and G. Fishelson
    1970   Inequality in income distribution. *Economic quarterly* 17:75–88 (Hebrew).

Yuchtman-Yaar, E., and M. Semyonov
    1979   Ethnic inequality in Israel: Schools and sports: An expectation state approach. *American journal of sociology* 85:576–90.

Zakai, D.
    1985   *Economic development in Judea-Samaria and the Gaza District, 1981–82*. Jerusalem: Bank of Israel Research Department.

Zuker, D., A. Halprin, Z. Hasper, H. Kahana, and R. Levin
    1983   *Human rights in the territories occupied by the Israel defence force*. Jerusalem: International Center for Peace in the Middle East.

Index